AUSCHWITZ

A Doctor's Story

Translated from the German by
Susan Ray

With an Introduction by
Deborah Lipstadt

Historical advice and annotations by
Arthur J. Slavin

AUSCHWITZ
A Doctor's Story

Lucie Adelsberger

NORTHEASTERN UNIVERSITY PRESS
Boston

Women's Life Writings from Around the World
Edited by Marilyn Yalom

Northeastern University Press

Library of Congress Cataloging-in-Publication Data
Adelsberger, Lucie, 1895–
[Auschwitz. English]
Auschwitz : a doctor's story / Lucie Adelsberger ; translated from the German by Susan Ray ; with an introduction by Deborah Lipstadt ; and historical advice and annotations by Arthur J. Slavin.
p.   cm.—(Women's life writings from around the world)
Translation of: Auschwitz : ein Tatsachenbericht.
Includes bibliographical references.
ISBN 1-55553-233-0 (cl : alk. paper)—ISBN 1-55553-250-0 (pbk.)
1. Adelsberger, Lucie, 1895–   .   2. Jews—Germany—Berlin—Biography. 3. Jewish physicians—Germany—Berlin—Biography. 4. Holocaust, Jewish (1939–1945)—Personal narratives.   5. Auschwitz (Poland : Concentration camp)   6. World War, 1939–1945—Gypsies—Poland.   7. Berlin (Germany)—Biography.   I. Slavin, Arthur Joseph.   II. Title.   III. Series.
DS135.G5A33313   1995
940.53'18'092—dc20
[B]   95-20764

Designed by Diane Levy

Composed in Minion by Graphic Composition, Athens, Georgia. Printed and bound by Thomson-Shore, Inc., Dexter, Michigan. The paper is Glatfelter Supple Opaque Recycled, an acid-free stock.

MANUFACTURED IN THE UNITED STATES OF AMERICA
99 98 97 96 95   5 4 3 2 1

PREFACE

THIS REPORT tells the story of the victims of Auschwitz, not with the purpose of opening old wounds, but of passing it on as a legacy for us Jews and for all mankind. It will fulfill its purpose only if it helps teach us, who call ourselves the children of God, to become better human beings, to truly love our neighbors, and to work toward the eradication of brutality from the face of the earth.

—LUCIE ADELSBERGER

CONTENTS

List of Illustrations ix

Introduction by Deborah Lipstadt xiii

◆ PART ONE ◆

The Trap 3

The Housing Crisis 5

Fear 9

Praying for the Death of One's Parents 10

Him or Me 12

The Alien City 13

◆ PART TWO ◆

The Shrill Whistle 21

Stripped of Everything 26

The Gypsy Camp 30

Mulo, Mulo 35

Sunday in the Camp 41

Hunger 43

Roll Call 46

Typhus 50

CONTENTS

◆ **PART THREE** ◆

Candy for the Little Ones   57
The Dentist   60
On Death   62
Why?   67
Kohinoor   68
Curds and Whey   70
Das Sonderkommando   73
The Pilgrimage to Death   80
In the Sauna   85
Gypsy Night   86

◆ **PART FOUR** ◆

The Mother and the Grandmother   95
Motherhood   100
Between the Spheres   102
Mala, the Belgian Woman   103
A Broken Leg   104
Two Hungarians   106
Behind the Fence   108

◆ **PART FIVE** ◆

A Hike through the Snow   119
Disgust   126
The Liberation   128
Looking Back (Summer 1946)   131

Notes   137

ILLUSTRATIONS

Diagram of Auschwitz-Birkenau   xi

Map of Auschwitz and environs   24

Selection   25

The main guardhouse   27

New women prisoners   29

A women's barracks   37

Roll call   46

Hair of murdered women   64

The "Canada" commando greets new arrivals   74

Sorting "Canada" property   77

The arrival of Hungarian Jews   81

Awaiting selection   82

Women and children selected for death   84

Aerial view of Birkenau   110

Arbeit Macht Frei   120

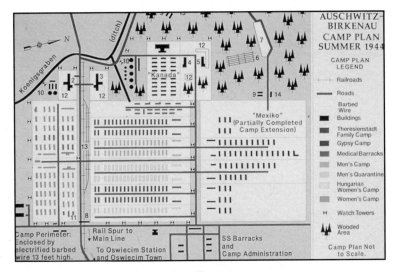

Key

1. "Sauna" (disinfection)
2. Gas chamber and Crematorium No. 2
3. Gas chamber and Crematorium No. 3
4. Gas chamber and Crematorium No. 4
5. Gas chamber and Crematorium No. 5
6. Cremation pits
7. Mass graves for Soviet POWs
8. Main guardhouse
9. Barracks for disrobing
10. Sewage plant
11. Medical experiments barracks
12. Buried ashes from crematoria
13. Railroad platform
14. Provisional gas chamber no. 1
15. Provisional gas chamber no. 2

INTRODUCTION

DURING HIS FINAL DAYS in the Riga ghetto, the illustrious Jewish historian Solomon Dubnow is reported to have told every Jew he met: "Write it down. Record it."[1] And that is what myriad survivors have done. There is much we do not know about an event that—no matter how many memoirs or historical works are ultimately produced—will forever remain beyond our complete comprehension. Each story adds a piece to the puzzle; every vignette gives us a better grasp of it. Anyone who reads Lucie Adelsberger's memoir will come away having learned a great deal about what it was like to be an inmate, a doctor, and a woman in Auschwitz. But that is not all there is here. Her memoir, first published in German in 1956 and out of print in that language for many years, provides powerful insights into both life in Berlin during the Nazi period and life in Auschwitz/

---

1. Israel Gutman, "Simon Dubnow," *Encyclopedia of the Holocaust* (New York, 1990), pp. 408–9.

Birkenau.[2] Adelsberger demonstrates what it was to have tried to remain a human being in such a setting.

In the not too distant future these Holocaust memoirs, which today seem so plentiful, will seem to be precious few. For they—together with the growing storehouse of video interviews—will have to replace a resource that we still have at present (though sadly not in Adelsberger's case): today, fifty years after the liberation of the camps, we still have among us some of the survivors, irreplaceable and unique. Many have already died. Within a short time those who can speak with firsthand knowledge of the camps will no longer be here to sit before the camera, talk to our classes, deliver speeches, and give oral testimony. Future generations will not hear the story from people who can say, "This is what happened to *me*. This is *my* story." For them it will be part of the distant past and, consequently, easier to revise, deny, or—most tragic of all—forget. Then the survivors' memoirs will be of even greater importance. Although Adelsberger's recollections may initially stand out from the others because of her unusual situation as a doctor, it is her ability to convey in a simple and understated fashion the impact of the maelstrom in which she was trapped that makes this work particularly powerful.

◆ ◆ ◆

PRIOR TO THE WAR Adelsberger (1895–1971) lived in Berlin, where she served for twenty years as a physician specializing in immunology and allergies. In addition to maintaining a private practice, she conducted research at the Robert Koch Institute and published her find-

---

2. Adelsberger was not deported from Berlin until the relatively late date of May 1943. She was witness, therefore, to the almost total dismantling of what had been one of the world's great Jewish communities.

INTRODUCTION

ings in a wide variety of medical journals. Her articles and mono-
graphs brought her work to the attention of colleagues in many other
countries, including the United States. She was among a growing
number of women, many of them Jewish, who during the Weimar
Republic trained and served as doctors. By the time the Nazis came
to power, 3,376 of the 51,527 doctors in Germany were women.[3]
More than 20 percent of Germany's female physicians were in Berlin.[4] Many of these women held low-status positions in public health
clinics and social health services. While some women chose this area
of medical practice because of its personal and political rewards,
many found themselves relegated to it because of insurmountable
barriers placed in their paths by the medical establishment, their
families, and societal hostility toward women professionals. Which
prevented their entering more lucrative and prestigious fields. Adelsberger distinguished herself from her female colleagues: she was able
to achieve the "higher ranks of the profession," that is, she was able
both to maintain a private practice and to gain entrée into academic
medicine.[5] She had an international reputation long before her deportation. In fact, Harvard offered her a prominent faculty position
in bacteriology in 1933. But she rejected that invitation because she
could not obtain a visa for her mother, whom she would have had to
leave behind.

---

3. *Die Arztin* 9 (December 1933): 260–61, as cited in Atina Grossman, "German Women Doctors from Berlin to New York: Maternity and Modernity in
Weimar and in Exile," *Feminist Studies* 19, no. 1 (Spring 1993): 67.

4. Of the 722 women doctors in Berlin, 270 were Jews. *Die Arztin* 11 (September 1935): 148, as cited in Grossman, "German Women Doctors," p. 67.

5. Grossman, "German Women Doctors," p. 67.

INTRODUCTION

With the Nazis' ascent to power, life changed markedly for all Jewish doctors. The changes were, of course, ominous.[6] Within two months Jewish doctors faced boycotts and individual acts of terror. Eventually they were excluded from national health insurance programs and barred from treating anyone but Jews. Adelsberger was able to maintain her medical practice in Berlin, although during the years immediately prior to her deportation she could no longer call herself a doctor. The Nazis withdrew that title from her and her Jewish colleagues; instead, she became a *Judenbehandler,* an attendant of Jews. In the first six months of 1943 massive deportations took place from Berlin. Among the last Jews to be deported, she was placed on a transport on May 17, 1943.[7]

---

6. Things changed for women doctors as well. The number of women doctors decreased markedly as a result of the Nazi preference for women to remain out of the work force. The outbreak of war and the absence of "non-Aryan" doctors eventually reversed this trend and many women returned to the practice of medicine.

Jewish women doctors who expected other women doctors to come to their defense were, by and large, bitterly disappointed. The League of German Women Doctors accepted Nazi *Gleichschaultung* (racial and political purification) and in the spring of 1933 expelled its Jewish members. Michael H. Kater, *Doctors under Hitler* (Chapel Hill, N.C., 1989), pp. 108, 92–93; Grossman, "German Women Doctors," p. 82.

7. Apparently, because of her medical expertise she was kept off the deportation lists until one of the final transports. The last deportations from Berlin actually took place in early 1945, but by that time there was only a handful of Jews left in the city. Between 1941 and 1945 a total of sixty-three transports left Berlin for extermination camps and 117 left for Theresienstadt. In all, approximately fifty thousand Jews were deported from the city. K. J. Ball-Kaduri, "Berlin is 'Purged' of Jews: The Jews in Berlin in 1943," *Yad Vashem Studies* 5 (1963): 271–316.

In Auschwitz Adelsberger was initially assigned to the sick ward of the Gypsy camp, where, without the aid of medical equipment or medicine, she tried to alleviate the inmates' suffering. There was little she could do for them. In fact, within less than a month of her arrival in the camp she contracted typhus.[8] Her service in the Gypsy portion of the camp continued until the "liquidation" of the Gypsies at the end of July 1944. After that she was assigned to care for a group of children in the women's camp at Birkenau. Once again, she was forced to be a pseudo-doctor, caring for these young people without medicine or even the most primitive equipment. Often, all she could do for them was help disguise their illness or their age so that they would not be selected for the gas chambers. Some of the children under her care were twins who were being used by Josef Mengele, the infamous camp physician at Auschwitz, for his sordid experiments. The juxtaposition of Mengele's use of his medical training to inflict pain and suffering on innocent victims with Adelsberger's attempt—absent the most basic tools of her profession—to alleviate suffering and preserve life demonstrates the diametrically opposed purposes to which medical skills could be put. In the world created by Germany's Third Reich medical training became a neutral tool: it could be used for the most diabolical or heroic of purposes.

As the Russians approached in January 1945, the SS took the approximately sixty thousand surviving prisoners and set out on the

---

8. A few years after her arrival in the United States she wrote an article analyzing her bout with typhus and her willingness to do everything in order to fight it through. Lucie Adelsberger, "Typhus Fever in Auschwitz Concentration Camp," in *When Doctors Are Patients,* ed. Max Pinner and Benjamin F. Miller (New York, 1952), pp. 178–82.

infamous "death march." The Germans were determined that no prisoners survive to fall into the hands of the liberators and relate what had happened in Auschwitz. But the Germans simply did not have enough time to kill all those who still survived. So they gathered up the remaining prisoners and began to march them through the snow toward Germany.[9] They marched about 120 kilometers in horrendous conditions; they were then loaded on open coal cars and transported to Germany. Thousands who had survived Auschwitz perished on the march. Those who survived this ordeal were dispersed to a number of different camps, including Gross-Rosen, Buchenwald, Dachau, Mauthausen, and Ravensbrück. After a harrowing ordeal, Adelsberger's group eventually reached Ravensbrück. At the very end of the war she was moved from Ravensbrück to a town called Neustadt, where she was liberated.

◆ ◆ ◆

ALL SURVIVOR MEMOIRS connect us in varying degrees to the past. But there are some that are exceptional because they transmit the experience in a fashion that helps us vicariously experience—as much as is possible—both the extent to which the Germans managed to degrade people even before they killed them and the way in which many (though certainly not all) of the victims found in themselves the strength and resolve to maintain both their dignity and their hope. Adelsberger's is such a memoir. It touches us in many powerful ways. First of all, she provides an oddly colorful description of life in

---

9. The weakest prisoners were not taken on the march. Apparently, the Germans planned to kill the remaining prisoners before leaving the camp but fled without doing so. The Russian forces found approximately six thousand prisoners alive in the camp when they arrived.

the Gypsy camp at Auschwitz. Demonstrating how different it was from other sections of Auschwitz, she paints a vivid portrait of the variety show the Gypsies managed to stage in the midst of this death factory. For a short while both the participants and the audience were able to lose themselves in the illusion of normalcy: gymnasts formed high pyramids, clowns cavorted, musicians played violins and an accordion, and onlookers danced. This moment of joy and celebration ended abruptly with the order for all inmates to return to their blocks immediately. Later, as darkness fell, the SS came and took twenty-five hundred Czech Gypsies to the gas chambers. Adelsberger then understood that this carnival, with all its joy and laughter, was but a prelude to Auschwitz's leitmotif, death.

Adelsberger witnessed the end of the Gypsy camp, describing in vivid detail the refusal of the Gypsy children to go submissively to their deaths. They kick, scream, and fight ferociously, shouting "murderers" at the SS officers who came to take them away. They knew what awaited them, and they would not go quietly.

But Adelsberger's contribution is not just in painting the historical details. The greatness of this memoir lies in her ability to capture the ultimate import of even the most prosaic moment. She does this in the pre-Auschwitz as well as the Auschwitz portion of her work. She conveys the way the Nazis managed to rob Jews of their dignity long before they reached the camps. On the very first page she writes about the July 1938 Gestapo edict permitting Jews to sit only on those benches reserved specifically for them. Most scholars who write about the Holocaust tend to treat such regulations as of relatively minor importance when compared to the far more significant prohibitions Jews faced. But this prohibition had severe consequences, particularly for one segment of the population. Jewish benches generally were few and far between, and, moreover, someone sitting on one instantly opened himself or herself to ridicule or assault from passersby. Adelsberger rightly observes that such a prohibition might seem trivial, given the many other terrible travails the Jews faced. But it was, in fact, quite extreme for elderly Jews, who in 1938 formed a disproportionately large sector of the remaining German Jewish population. Left behind by younger generations and without sufficient strength to stroll through their neighborhoods, the elderly often considered a brief respite on a park bench the high point of their day. Now, Adelsberger observes, they were "deprived of this pleasure, too, for the Jews were begrudged the very air they breathed."

Adelsberger's personal situation infused her observations about the trials of the elderly with a particular poignancy: her mother was one of those who could no longer leisurely stroll in the park and sit where she wished. Her relationship with her mother forms a critical element of her story. She captures in vivid emotional detail the dilemma faced by those German Jews who were young enough to build new lives elsewhere and lucky enough to have the opportunity to do so, but whose parents were neither. Should these children abandon those who had given them life, particularly if the parents were weak and ill and depended on their children for subsistence? On several occasions Adelsberger chose not to. Her mother was her anchor to Germany. If not for her devotion to her mother she would certainly have escaped the fate she describes so vividly in this memoir. She turned down a number of opportunities to emigrate because her mother could not get a visa to accompany her. Adelsberger was in the United States in November 1938 at the time of Kristallnacht. Shortly thereafter President Roosevelt issued an Executive Order permitting those Germans then in the United States on visitors' visas to remain in the country if returning placed them in a precarious situation. Under the terms of this decision, Adelsberger could probably have remained here, safe from harm's way. Given her international reputation, she would probably have found a position in this country. Moreover, she had close relatives who would have provided her with shelter.[10] However, her concern about leaving her elderly mother alone in Berlin led her to return to Germany. She left her personal papers in America when she departed, obviously aware that she was returning to a situation that boded no good.

As a doctor Adelsberger faced yet another dilemma. She saw how elderly Jews were treated by the Gestapo when it was their turn to be deported. They were humiliated and forced to endure conditions that even those far younger found unbearable. On occasion, adult children who were caring for their parents were deported, leaving the elderly parents behind without the support system necessary for their survival. Adelsberger was in a unique situation. She had access to medication that would have allowed her mother, a stroke victim, a peaceful end rather than a potentially horrifying death. The knowledge that she could "liberate" her mother from this possibility drove her "half mad." She wondered, "Am I supposed to kill my mother, the person most dear to me in all the world?" In one sentence she captures the power of the Nazis' depravity to turn the world upside down. An entire generation of German Jews, Adelsberger observed, knew but one prayer: the wish for "the death of our parents." Within

---

10. According to a cousin of Adelsberger, her relatives were required to put up $500 in order to get her off of Ellis Island when she arrived in the United States. She was released the next day.

a few short years the Nazis had transformed the "most sacred bond into a death wish."

This was not the only way the Nazis turned nature on its head. In Auschwitz Adelsberger and her medical colleagues in the women's camp were responsible for the pregnancy block. They saved whatever poisons they could find in order to kill newborn children immediately. Not to have done so would have been to condemn the child *and* the mother to certain death in the gas chambers. Doctors who had been trained to preserve life had to become killers in order to help their patients survive. At the same time and in the same place, Mengele, who had the same training as these doctors, was using his knowledge to inflict severe and sadistic pain on his patients.

Writing about life—and death—in the Gypsy camp, Adelsberger observed that it offered a number of unofficial amenities unavailable in the rest of Birkenau. Cooking, Adelsberger observes, was forbidden. That did not stop the inmates for, as Adelsberger notes wryly, living was not allowed either and they tried that as well.

There is another aspect of Adelsberger's work that increases its significance: it allows us to hear the voice of a woman survivor of Auschwitz. We have far too few memoirs that tell the specific stories of women. Much of the best survivor literature by women is out of print or not available in English translation.[11] But more important, perhaps, is the fact that historical works on the Holocaust tend to

---

11. Carol Rittner and John K. Roth, eds., *Different Voices: Women and the Holocaust* (New York, 1993), p. xi.

present this event as if victims' gender differences were irrelevant.[12] They universalize the experience of the male victim to all victims. Many excellent historians write about "Jewish victims" but are in fact writing about Jewish *male* victims, seemingly unaware that what happened to the women was often quite different from what happened to the men. This is not to suggest that what was done to women was worse than what was done to men, merely that it was *different*. To tell the story of the male experience as if it were the experience of *all* prisoners is to render the ultimate injustice to the women victims of the Nazis: it is to make them invisible and render their experience irrelevant.[13]

Some of the differences between men's and women's experiences are strikingly illustrated by Adelsberger. Unlike Jewish men, Jewish women were killed not solely because they were Jews but also because they had the ability to produce another generation of Jews to replace those being destroyed by the Nazis. Heinrich Himmler felt obligated to offer special justification for the killing of the women (no justification was needed for killing Jewish men): "We came to the question: what about the women and children? I have decided to find a clear solution here too. In fact I did not regard myself as justified in exterminating the men—let us say killing them or having them killed— while letting avengers in the shape of the children . . . grow up. The

---

12. Joan Ringelheim, "Women and the Holocaust: A Reconsideration of Research," in *Different Voices*, ed. Rittner and Roth, p. 392.

13. Myrna Goldenberg, "Different Horrors, Same Hell: Women Remembering the Holocaust," in *Thinking the Unthinkable: Meanings of the Holocaust*, ed. Roger S. Gottlieb (New York, 1991), pp. 150–66.

difficult decision had to be taken to make this people disappear from the face of the earth."[14] Women bore a double liability: they were Jews and they were women, and that made them particularly dangerous enemies of the Germans. Jewish children arriving in the camps were generally killed immediately; in order to maintain the charade of relocation and keep the children and their parents calm, the mothers were sent with their young ones to the gas chambers. Veteran prisoners sometimes tried to place young children in line next to their grandmothers or other older women. Both would automatically be condemned to death because of their ages. Mothers unaccompanied by children might be able to survive. As Adelsberger observes, "every Jewish child automatically condemned his mother to death." Even a woman who happened to be with a child not her own when she alighted from the train and stood in line before Mengele faced a good chance of being sent to her death with the child. Women with children were, Joan Ringelheim observes, among the most vulnerable people in the camps. Only children alone were in a more vulnerable situation.[15]

However, according to scholars who have examined the particular ordeal of women victims of the Nazis, women who lived in the camps had at least one advantage over the men. Many women were able to create surrogate "families":[16] small groups of two or more inmates who would take care of each other. They used their nurturing skills

---

14. Bradley F. Smith and Agnes F. Peterson, eds., *Heinrich Himmler: Geheimreden 1933 bis 1945* (Frankfurt, 1974), as quoted in Ringelheim, "Women and the Holocaust," p. 392.

15. Ringelheim, "Women and the Holocaust," p. 378.

16. Ibid.

to help each other survive. Adelsberger's story repeatedly confirms this point. Not only did she nurture others, particularly her patients, but at one point two young girls to whom she had become quite close adopted her as their "camp mother." Though she was the oldest in the "family," the girls ended up taking care of her. Together they would sit at night and talk about what they would do when they emerged from Auschwitz—even though none believed they would— in order to prevent a second Auschwitz. According to Adelsberger, they were not the only women to create a surrogate family: "Everyone had her own." Motivated by a need for solidarity and a feeling of responsibility for others who shared their fate, these women formed deep friendships. The love and support that came with these relationships "eased the horrors of their miserable end."

Lucie Adelsberger's memoir cannot help stirring readers deeply. Both those who know much about the Holocaust and those who know little will be moved by this small but truly important book. She has made a significant contribution to depicting life—if one can call it that—in the hell that was Auschwitz.

Atlanta   DEBORAH E. LIPSTADT
March 1995

• PART ONE •

The Trap

IT BEGAN WITH only a few so-called "trifles"—small matters, to be sure, but of such consequence they may not be overlooked.

The first: In July of 1938, the Gestapo published an edict, brief and so inconspicuous it was hardly noticed among the mass and welter of otherwise grave and vital regulations. It announced that Jews in public places were permitted to sit only on the benches specifically reserved for them, and nowhere else. Despite the few "Jewish benches" here and there, a prohibition such as this seemed almost ludicrous to people whose minds were occupied with serious concerns: people who had been just about eliminated from social and professional life and who were being driven out of their homes and onto the streets from one day to the next by overzealous, Nazi-sympathizing landlords.[1] Nevertheless, this ordinance was radical enough: many of the Jews still living in Germany were elderly people no longer able to begin a new life in another country; thus, they found it difficult to summon the necessary enthusiasm the younger generation needed to support their own attempts to start over. These old folks had to be left behind—in small apartments, in boarding houses, in little back rooms—burdened by the eternal indifference of the physically infirm. Bored and lacking initiative, they dragged themselves through the day under the dead weight of monotony. A brief respite on a park bench watching children play, listening to the birds, and enjoying the gardens formed the high point of the day for these people who no longer had the strength to spend the hour strolling through the neighborhood. Now they were being deprived of this pleasure, too, for the Jews were begrudged the very air they breathed.

The second instance took place on the Kurfürstenstraße in Berlin about one year later, in June of 1939. The Gestapo had enthroned themselves there in what previously had been a Masonic lodge. The building was now one large bureaucracy where they issued the necessary papers required for passports and emigration.[2] On the whole, the scene was that of a heavily besieged agency where crowds of people waited hours on end for their processing. The only remarkable thing was that these masses were interspersed with the aged and the infirm, and never was a chair or some other seating arrangement provided for them. I was there with my elderly mother, who had a provisionary visa to—Honolulu, let's say. (I realize this respectable country should not be abused in this pseudonymous way.)* After a four-hour wait, we finally made it to the large hall where the various functionaries of the Gestapo, each posted at a different table, performed their weighty functions and set their signatures, at once automatically and authoritatively, to the identification papers. As we were being herded along from one table to another, wedged in as we were amidst the crowd, my mother, this kindly woman, smiled warmly at the official who had just dealt with her business. He looked at her with a livid expression and shouted: "You dare to smile? You'll soon forget about laughing. We'll see to that!" That's when I realized that these people were beyond the reach of human kindness.

The third occurrence happened eight days later at the office of the consul to "Honolulu." I went there on business having to do with my mother's visa. For months I had fought, worried, and agonized over this visa, which would have allowed her to leave Germany.[3] I wrote my fingers to the bone filling out the necessary forms. During the day I ran from one office to another, besieging them all; during the

---

* This is probably a covert reference to Switzerland; see note 2 on this point.

night, since I couldn't sleep, I raged through the streets and counted the cobblestones in the moonlight, ready to dig up each and every one of them with my bare hands if such an act would have served any purpose. I finally had the passport and the provisionary visa in hand. With chest held high and fully conscious of the fact that I had succeeded, I hurried to the consul and raced up the stairs. Half an hour later I was on the stairs again and knew, for the first time, what people mean when they say their knees turned to jelly or the rug had been pulled out from under their feet. I hadn't succeeded; the consul denied the visa. The reason given: a small detail, a minor proviso that did not satisfy the regulations.

As an isolated case, this incident would have been entirely uninteresting and of significance only to us, but as a representative example, it is one of many. Thousands hoped, worried, trembled, waited, stood on their heads, ran around in circles, and still ended up empty-handed, all because—and this, too, was something we had to add to what we already knew—the *outside* world didn't want to get involved.[4]

The Housing Crisis

FRAU X., the director of the Jewish Advisory Board for Housing in Berlin,[5] was summoned to appear before the Gestapo in August of 1941. Rumor had it that she returned pale and exhausted. Cynics dismissed the incident with a smile: another rumor and another demonstration of how quickly myths grow up around "public" figures. Why should a meeting with the Gestapo, a weekly occurrence, at the least, in the course of her duties—why should such a meeting upset Frau X., a woman with nerves of steel, one whom years of training in police service had hardened to take all surprises with equanimity and to resist all sentiment with indifference? Had it been otherwise, she wouldn't have been able to perform her duties as head of the Jewish Advisory Board for Housing—especially at a time when it was considered good form to drive Jews out of their homes in order to "cleanse" the buildings, all the while being simultaneously forbidden to direct these newly created homeless to compensatory apartments in so-called Aryan buildings. They weren't allowed to sleep on the street, either, with the result that the remaining Jewish apartments were exploited to the fullest, sheltering as many families as could fit. Nevertheless, Frau X. was reported to have acquiesced during her secret meeting to the Gestapo demand that she deliver even more apartments "free of Jews" and accommodate the inhabitants elsewhere. Some people held this against her.

Approximately two weeks later one thousand to twelve hundred families received a letter with the following announcement: "Your apartment has been designated for evacuation. You are required [or did it say 'requested'?] to submit a list of all furniture as well as all personal property to the Advisory Board for Housing." The enormous number of these notices in one fell swoop seemed to surpass even Frau X.'s fears. She, whom even her enemies credited with integrity and a willingness to help others, could do nothing to relocate a thousand extended families together with all their subtenants. The impatiently insistent were told they had to wait. Rumors were rampant about tent cities on the outskirts of Berlin and about the establishment of a ghetto,[6] while the eternal optimists whispered something about an empty threat to intimidate the Jews. The only sure thing was the fact that the Advisory Board for Housing did nothing beyond comforting those who received such a letter; it even failed to grant them the requisite permission to move, in the rare instance when they did manage to find some form of shelter on their own.

Weeks passed, full of the distress and anxiety a person feels when he doesn't know where he might rest his weary bones the next day or maybe even that very evening and accompanied by all the nervous manifestations such insecurity engenders. However, one adjusts to everything eventually, and a new rumor flared up in mid-October. Through a leak in high places it was learned that the Gestapo were planning another raid on the Jews for October 16th. The 30th of July was still a vivid memory for all of us, the date the Gestapo had once before staged an evening excursion and sent hundreds of people to the labor camp at Wuhlheide.* Whoever wasn't found at home at the prescribed time, the stroke of nine in the evening, or was still "strolling around" the streets at that time, was sent off.

Even if only a temporary detention, thirty days in a labor camp with all its rigors is a drastic punishment for tardiness, and it left a deep impression. The broken bones and festering wounds suffered by the few who returned alive from Wuhlheide only to vegetate in a hospital proved a very effective tool for teaching punctuality. Orderly and obedient, on the evening of October 16, 1940, all Jews were at home, even the few who otherwise might have dared to undertake an evening escapade.[7]

The next morning was alive with reports that the Gestapo really had been at work. All the apartments falling under the evacuation order had been evacuated. In the dark of night—inconspicuously, as

---

* Wuhlheide is a hamlet about twelve kilometers east of Berlin's suburban ring, on the River Wuhle. It was the site of a so-called "protective camp."

was their way, for the Gestapo preferred to do their deeds at night so as not to arouse too much of an audience as well as to escape admiration for their zeal—in the dark of night, then, between nine and midnight, young and old, healthy and sick, even those hardly able to stagger along, were dragged out of their homes with whatever essentials they had been able to gather together at the last moment. They were led to the closest police station to register their departure (in keeping with the law as befits an efficient nation-state) and then interned in the synagogue on Levetzowstraße. Before they could gather any further information, they were transported away. Postcards later revealed their destination as Litzmannstadt—Łódź.*

That's how the housing shortage was solved.

And that's how it all began in Berlin. Not long before that the Stettiner Jews had been transported away as the result of "an isolated incident of an overzealous District Leader," as the saying went. Even when the Jews from Baden were deported to Gurs** in the south of France in October of 1940, things still didn't seem all that bad. The same scene was repeated again and again in almost every city in Europe under Gestapo rule—in Warsaw and Oslo,[8] in Amsterdam, in Brussels, in Paris, in Thessalonika—and everywhere, the new actors were astonished at the role they were forced to play.

---

* Łódź, a Polish industrial city about 130 kilometers southwest of Warsaw, had its name changed to Litzmannstadt on September 8, 1939, when it fell to Nazi forces. The name honored General Karl Litzmann, who had taken the city in World War I.

** The first detention camp in France set up by the pro-Nazi Vichy Government. Originally a camp for defeated Spanish antifascists, Gurs, about eighty kilometers from the Spanish frontier, became a camp for Jews in 1940.

Fear

FEAR CLINGS to the walls in your bedroom, crawls along the floor, and drips down from the ceiling; when you cross the threshold of your home, fear seizes you at the door and embraces you in an inescapable net; it hangs around in alleys and courtyards, lurking and waiting to attack as soon as you dare step out into the open. Fear is all around you, in all physical states—solid, liquid, gas; it presses in on you from without and seeps into you, and you have to hold it deep within yourself, silently, so as not to pass it on to others. It persists—in the night it wipes the sleep from your tired eyes, and during the day, on all following days and for all the weeks and months to come, it persists, without pause, without slack. Fear has a beginning but no end; it reaches a climax but never becomes a habit. Its corroding effect increases not arithmetically, but geometrically.

How can anyone imagine what it's like to tremble at the arrival of the mail (three deliveries a day), fully expecting a summons to appear before the Gestapo or a letter from the Jewish Council inviting you, in accordance with its official list, to evacuate on such and such a date—you and your husband or your parents or your son, one after the other of all whom your heart holds dear? Or can anyone imagine what an instrument of torture the doorbell can become when your every nerve is strained from morning to night listening for it, and when its imagined ringing startles you out of deepest sleep? When the Hitler Youth pull on it already at dawn to prepare you for a visit from the Gestapo? And when, late at night, it shatters the silence and heralds a sadistic housemaster who just happens to know the rhythm of your fear and gloats in taking advantage of it?

Fear defined the life of the "politically unreliable elements" as well as that of every Jew wherever Hitler set his foot. Whoever hasn't experienced every hypersensitive nerve in his body attuned to being hunted down in this way doesn't know what fear is.

Fear is the antechamber to hell.

Praying for the Death of One's Parents

To the Memory of Our Beloved Mother

ALTHOUGH SHOCKED and already wincing under the first tentative lightning bolts of the Hitler regime, we had not yet foreseen the coming storm of annihilation. In those early days, the wrenching separation of parents from their children who were emigrating to foreign lands seemed monstrous to us. Many young people remained simply because they were unable to face this separation, especially since it seemed nothing short of final, and they didn't want to abandon their helpless parents. They were still there when the manhunts began, and most of them paid for their loyalty with their lives without having been able to help anyway. This has to be said, clearly and unequivocally, for those who did go and who, out of ignorance of the situation and inappropriate remorse, spent sleepless nights writhing under the pangs of conscience; and it has to be said for those who continue to torture themselves with senseless reproaches. No one could help anyone else, not even by putting his own life on the line. Children watched as their parents were led away, and parents had to stand by while their children, to whom they clung, were dragged from them. If they happened to be present at the sudden seizure and if the Gestapo functionaries were so inclined, they were allowed to help with the packing and share a last embrace. That was it.

I loved my mother very much and returned to Germany again and again on her account. When she fell sick, I let my last chance for emigration pass by unheeded. She had had a stroke and lay paralyzed in bed, unable to sit up or even to turn over by herself. She needed help with every bite she took and every sip she drank. She had a devoted nurse who cared for her during the day; I came in the evening after office hours were over and I had finished my house calls. In her quiet room we were able to keep my mother ignorant of any news about the deportation of the Jews, but while I sat at her bedside and chatted about my practice, passing the time with pleasantries and amusements, I tensed at every sound at the door, every step in the stairwell, and every car that stopped in front of the house. When would they come and take us away, together or separately? Would they take me alone and leave my sick mother lying helplessly behind, or would they take her as a prisoner to some hospital where I would no longer be allowed to visit? I knew what had happened to the renowned bacteriologist Dr. H., who was confined to his bed with a festering knee infection and was being cared for by his devoted and self-sacrificing daughter. One evening the Gestapo took them both away. First, the daughter disappeared into a detention camp and then to the next transport,[9] never to be seen again. Her father's turn came later. Toward midnight he was loaded onto a small van, an open and jolting vehicle meant for cargo, and driven under pouring rain to the hospital. Once there, like all the others destined for evacuation, he was treated as a prisoner and locked in his room like a common criminal. Only physicians and nurses had access; in all the months preceding his death no one else was allowed to see him; no letter, no greeting could reach him.

Was I supposed to abandon my mother to a similar fate? I had the means at my disposal—one swallow, one injection—that would spare her such an end. Many people actually did manage to give their parents some liberating sedative. I found comfort in the thought at first, but then, when the roundups increased and the time came ever nearer, I began to waver. Finally, the mere thought of it drove me half mad. Was I, who had spent her whole life struggling to save each and every human life, was I supposed to kill my mother, the person most dear to me in all the world? May a person who trusts in a higher power ever deliberately end a life, be it her own or that of another? I couldn't do it.

But I did get on my knees and beseech God to let my mother die before the thugs could drag her away with their murderous hands. And I wasn't the only one—many sons and daughters did the same. We all knew but one prayer: the death of our parents. No human court can ever call the guilty to account for the emotional torment children suffered on behalf of their parents, a torture that transformed this most sacred bond into a death wish.

Him or Me

MANY OF MY longtime patients gradually became loyal friends, and we helped each other out through the years of fear and anguish. At the most inopportune moment, when the transports were chasing one another as if on a conveyor belt, one such friend managed to contract a severe gastric hemorrhage of the type that manifests itself in several stages and ceases, if at all, only a few days later. Such a hemorrhage always presents a dire threat, but at that critical time, when consideration was nothing more than an empty word, it was catastrophic. Even so, after three weeks the man improved, although he did remain bedridden. And in bed was where the Gestapo found him during one of their roundups. He was not "transportable" and was of no use in a labor camp, either, when that possibility came up. I insisted they call in the Jewish physician responsible for determining a person's suitability for deportation. The man who came was a young, very self-important doctor who positively radiated authority. He examined the patient thoroughly, listened to his heart and lungs, felt his abdomen, strode back and forth in the room a few times, hemmed and hawed a bit, and finally spoke up and declared the man able to go. I couldn't believe my ears and took the man aside to ask whether he actually meant what he had said. Gazing at me with a wan expression lacking all signs of his previous vainglory, he took his time before rasping: "It's him or me. One of us has to go." He had already been reprimanded for deferring too many people. To be a physician was a farce as soon as one became an unwilling minion of the Gestapo.

As a reward for his services, this colleague was sent to the East[10] a short time later, where he eventually shared the fate of his patients who had preceded him.

The Alien City

ON MAY 6TH they put me in the detention camp in the Groß-Hamburgerstraße between Rosenthalerplatz and Alexanderplatz.[11] I had been living in Berlin for twenty years by then and knew nothing of this Groß-Hamburgerstraße, not to mention the house in which we were interned. But that was my fault, because it was no ordinary house. Had I been a tourist in some foreign city, where I would have spent the very first day seeking out every ancient tomb, every venerable ruin, and the devotional mosaics of stained glass windows, it would never have escaped my notice. The house dated back to the

eighteenth century, and located behind it was the oldest Jewish cemetery in Berlin, where Moses Mendelssohn* lay buried. It was a small
graveyard with very old, crumbling and deteriorated headstones; ivy
crept willfully down from the graves and arrogantly smothered the
untended lawn with its thick clumps of grass. The house itself was
an old-fashioned, neglected building that had once served as an
old folks' home. Boxed into it now were somewhere between a thousand and twelve hundred people. It seemed very crowded to us, with
twenty-five to thirty-five people in one average-sized room. In the
months and years to come, I often yearned for these rooms, which
were properly built and fitted out with windows, where it didn't rain
in and the water didn't collect in large puddles on a slimy floor;
where there were only bedbugs and no lice; where there was even a
water faucet for every hundred people, and where each person had
his or her own space and could stretch out and spread out as much as
they wanted to. In those days, though, as I said, it seemed unbearably
cramped with so many people in one house, not to mention all their
baggage as well. At the roundup, the Gestapo functionaries announced that each of us might bring along whatever we needed. The
condition that each had to carry his own made for the most difficult
decisions. No one likes to play Diogenes** and, as a rule, doesn't

---

* The celebrated German Jewish Enlightenment thinker (1729–1786), who
settled in Berlin. Within his Jewish heritage he wrote widely on literary, philo-
sophical, and religious questions. He was immortalized by Gotthold Lessing in
Nathan The Wise (1781).

** Diogenes of Sinope (died ca. 320 B.C.), the most famous of the Cynic phi-
losophers. He taught that self-sufficiency and liberation from dependence on
worldly goods were the natural way of life.

voluntarily abandon one's possessions. It's only when you have absolutely nothing that you realize how superfluous and how burdensome most things are. Only then do you learn what is truly important and how essential such little things as a toothbrush, a sewing needle, and a spoon are. Every knapsack was packed and repacked at least ten times over, every pocket was searched again and again and restuffed with the absolutely essential; and every single object was mentally weighed against its usefulness, only to be ultimately cast aside with a last painful glance before being rejected for good. How much fuss we made about our modest belongings, when later—but I don't want to get ahead of myself.

It was an anxious existence for this crowd of people who found themselves for the first time living in such close quarters, and yet there still reigned a good sense of cohesion. Everything was shared, from the marmalade jar that was smuggled in to the last can of sardines (each family got one little fish). Even such complicated problems as the opening and closing of the windows were solved amicably and to the satisfaction of thirty different individuals. At night the fresh air streamed into the overcrowded room through the wide-open windows, and the moon with its friendly round face kept watch over our slumbers.

Perhaps it wanted to comfort and embrace us the way it did the chestnut trees growing in the courtyard, with their towering crowns brushing against the rear windows of the third floor. If you sat on the window seat, you could actually reach out and touch the thick foliage, and the huge, five-lobed leaves wafted lightly back and forth; you were so close you could let them stroke your arm, softly and soothingly, like a mother trying to ward off all sorrow and despair. And the pink and white blossoms, so big and so close, shimmered luxuriantly as never before. Each individual blossom inclined toward the observer; artlessly it displayed its yellow calyx and uninhibitedly stretched out its pert filaments. A dense, green forest of leaves punctuated by luminous blossoms against a deep blue, springtime sky— that, too, was part of our prison. And none of it was reminiscent of Berlin, that vibrantly pulsing metropolis.

And yet I was to see, was to drive through, that city one more time. One night I was plagued by a screaming toothache, and next morning they sent me to a clinic—not me alone, but a whole group of people with pains and infirmities of all sorts. Some had to be bandaged, others were to see the eye or the ear doctor, many were scheduled for lung X-rays and tuberculosis examinations. Whoever had the slightest complaint was treated and restored as quickly as possible in order to arrive at the final destination in tip-top shape. We were loaded on and locked in the back of a truck, which drove us through the city; SS[12] stood guard at the front and rear. I don't know why that open prisoner van didn't take the most direct route to the hospital; instead, it made a wide detour on Unter den Linden and drove past the Brandenburg Gate, through the Tiergarten, and via Moabit straight through the center of Berlin. It was the same city that had been my home for twenty years and from which I reluctantly had torn myself away every time I had to leave. It had the same layout— the Victory Column, the public monuments were still standing; the lawns of the Tiergarten still sprawled, and the surrounding houses showed no signs of bomb damage. And yet, it was a completely different city. I knew the disillusionment I always felt with places I once had loved that had somehow lost their old appearance and were now more memory than reality. But this was something else, something much worse. It was the same city, all right, but it was no longer ours. There was no escape from, no getting out of, the truck. The streets no longer existed for prisoners of the SS. The park, where we used to go walking, was nothing more than a backdrop that quickly faded away. The house in which you used to live took on an inimical air; it let you pass, unmoved. And the people were different, too— no longer friends, but enemies. The Berlin I once had loved so much was gone. It had turned into a foreign city, even before Auschwitz.*

---

* The German name for the small Polish town Oświeçim, about sixty kilometers west of Kraków. See note 17 for further details on this largest of all labor and extermination camps, including the presence there of the *Frauensabteilung* (Women's Section).

• PART TWO •

The Shrill Whistle

THE SCENE is one of crowds of people stuffed in freight cars. On the afternoon of May 17, 1943 (it was a Monday), we had been expedited by truck from the detention camp to the train station, again under heavy SS guard. Not to one of the main train stations, but to the station in the Putlitzstraße, way out in the north of Berlin in the vicinity of the Virchow Hospital, where huge warehouses lined the canal and abandoned factories laid large-scale claim to the landscape, where only a few people lived and the approach road was mostly uninhabited, for, as was well known, the Gestapo liked to keep its doings out of the limelight. Close to a thousand of us were herded onto freight cars here, exactly the way the "Jewish atrocity propaganda" had described. (A short time before, and for the first and only time, a Jewish transport to Theresienstadt* had been sent off in Belgian railroad cars, second class.[13] The cars were officially photographed and the pictures featured in the weekly Ufa[14] newsreels with the caption: "This is the way the Jews travel." There followed a second picture, the familiar, overcrowded freight cars, with the caption: "And this is the way they claim to travel.")

We departed toward evening and rolled on nonstop for the next thirty-six hours or so. We didn't know where we were going, except that, according to our orientation, it was eastward. If we stood on our toes or climbed up on the baggage, we could look through the hatches and follow the landscape pretty closely. We passed the Spree

---

* The Czech fortress city of Terezin in northwest Bohemia, renamed and converted to a ghetto for "privileged Jews" from throughout Europe in October 1941. It was intended at first for Jews from the Greater Reich only.

Forest, Lausitz, Reichenbach, and all the other stations we used to note happily in earlier times when we steamed our way to the Riesengebirge for winter outings. By noon we had made a wide circle around Breslau.[15]

Our freight car is overcrowded, although not as chockablock as the others because it's a medical wagon. The air in the tightly sealed boxcar, which hadn't been opened since the departure, is suffocating and pestilential, the ventilation through the meager air holes so inadequate as to be unnoticeable. The pails of excrement are filled to overflowing and drip down their sides, and with every jolt of the train they spill over and splash on the people nearby who can't get out of the way because of the crush. The perimeter of the car is a barricade of baby carriages, for we have many infants in our group. They scream in their dirty diapers and refuse to be comforted because there's nothing to clean them up with and nothing to drink. The milk their parents brought along has soured in the bottle, and our small supply of water gave out a long time ago. Even the sick plead in vain for a drop to quench their thirst.

At the very last minute a few seriously ill persons were shoved in on stretchers. One had taken Veronal because her child lay in the hospital with scarlet fever and she didn't want to leave him behind. They pumped her stomach to make her vomit; now she's still drowsy and won't stop calling for her son. A man with a filthy wound on his leg, a convict, is moaning in pain and tossing about restlessly. An elderly lady with asthma coughs and gasps for breath, her face a bluish red. She came directly from the hospital where she'd been sleeping for weeks because she didn't want to leave her husband alone. There are many children here, too, including a two-year-old girl with her father, a strong and robust young man. The mother was taken months ago and the child is his one and only joy; he won't part from her. During the day he'll gladly go to work, even hard labor, and perhaps leave the child in a nursery group; in the evening he plans to care for her himself. The child looks out at the world through beaming blue eyes and totters from one person to another asking for a piece of sugar; then, sucking the sweet, she runs back to her father and climbs on his lap. Next to me and in front of the hatch are two young girls of ten and twelve, blissful. This is the first trip of their lives. They kept watch the whole night through, followed the wandering stars, marveled at the sickle of the waning moon, the way it crept behind the mountains; during the day they counted the villages and greeted the distant towers of Breslau. They take note of every river and every hill and never budge from their lookout.

It's the second evening now and we've already left Breslau far behind, or at least it seems we have. The train has halted frequently—twenty, thirty times; An agonizing, tormenting stop—rumors circulated, something about gassing the trains. Maybe it isn't a rumor, and they have stopped the train to let the gas pour in. If we'd only get wherever we're going; we can't hold out much longer. But we're still a long way off. The train drags itself deeper into the night, slowly, hesitantly, from time to time slowing down and then speeding up again as if unsure of its way and preferring to turn back. In the darkness we can just make out meadows and fields and scattered villages, sometimes so close that the muffled mooing of a sleepy cow reaches our ears. The hours mount up. Again and again we turn on our pocket lamps. Around midnight blast furnaces appear and huge cranes and brightly illuminated steel crates and, all around, captive balloons—an enormous, twenty-four-hour-a-day operation. That might be our new workplace. But the train, which has finally re-

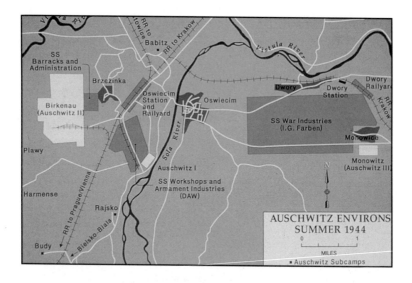

sumed a normal speed, hastens by, ever farther along, another half hour without interruption. Only then does it come to a final halt.

The shrill whistle of the locomotive shatters the night. We stare through the hatch. Everything is dark, except for the fact that the stars are twinkling. Another shrill whistle, piercing and penetrating, as if wanting to rouse the whole world out of its sleep. And then there was light. Spotlights shoot on, mighty reflectors flare up, the starry sky sinks back, and before our eyes lies a broad field, magically illuminated. We strain to see through the blinding brightness; masses of uniformed men bustle about, commands ring out, dogs bark. The blood flows in our veins as we recognize the SS insignia on the uniforms. "In the claws of the SS"—so this is what our new workplace looks like.

Upon arrival at Auschwitz-Birkenau, men and women were separated. Further divisions were made among the strong and the weak; the strong were selected for slave labor, the weak for immediate death in the gas chambers. In the top left of this photo can be seen the main guardhouse and watchtower, under which ran the railway line to the gas chambers and Crematoria II and III. Yad Vasham Photo Archives.

The doors of the boxcar are unbolted. "Get out! Quick!" Hurriedly we gather together the excessive baggage (how will we be able to carry it?) and climb out of the wagon. "Leave the baggage by the tracks!" is the second command and, relieved that we won't have to drag it around ourselves, we toss knapsack and suitcase next to the train. Immediately the men are herded away from the women and, separated from each other, are forced into columns with cuffs and blows. Then there starts the search for the sick—very careful and very thorough, but not very rigorous. The weak and the infirm, people over fifty-five and sometimes even over fifty, the children and all the women accompanied by children—none of them need stand in the rows any longer, for they're led off to the many trucks already waiting for them.[16] Twenty young people, prominent men and women distinguished in the fields of cultural and social work, are even called out by name and are granted the privilege of being the first to drive away. Only a small fraction of us, hardly a third, remains. Rude and vulgar zealots with harsh, metallic voices organize us quickly into five columns and march us off.

I heard that train whistle, that shrill, sharp whistle, just about every single night. It invaded my remotest dreams and wakened me from my deepest sleep. And whenever it did, I knew in my heart that another trainload of people were being unloaded in the glaring light of the railroad siding.

Stripped of Everything

FROM THE TRAIN STATION we marched at a brisk pace for about three kilometers; toward three in the morning we arrived in front of a large archway brightly flanked with glaring arc lamps. We were led into a fenced-in area surrounded by charged high-tension wires—the second shock of our highly personal reception by the SS. The tightly knit barbed wire stretched more than ten feet high in every direction, and placed at short intervals were signs warning of the high voltage

Stripped of Everything

This January 1945 photo shows the main guardhouse and entrance to Auschwitz-Birkenau, known to prisoners as the Gate of Death. National Museum of Auschwitz-Birkenau, Oświeçim, Poland, courtesy of the U.S. Holocaust Memorial Museum.

in the wire web. Two carts were jammed together in a ditch to the right of the gate, and in the bright lamplight we could just make out three black letters against a dark grey background: FKL.* A narrow wooden plank announced clearly and distinctly, again black against grey: Concentration Camp Auschwitz II.[17] No doubt remained; we now knew where we were, and the illusory promise the Gestapo had

---

* The letters *FKL* signify in German *Frauenskonzentrationslager* (Women's Concentration Camp). This large camp developed from the smaller *Frauensabteilung* established in 1940. See note 17.

made that we were heading for a labor camp vanished forever. (We later learned that this part of the camp was called Auschwitz Birkenau and encompassed the women's concentration camp, with approximately thirty thousand prisoners and five smaller camps with ten to twenty thousand prisoners each.)

SS women in grey uniforms swarmed out of a blockhouse to the left of the entrance and barked out orders for us to hand over our purses and bags; they then quickly and greedily gathered together what we knew to be the last of our possessions. The few remaining personal belongings we had so carefully and so traumatically salvaged and dragged along to Auschwitz, only to deposit them by the railroad siding, were, as we darkly comprehended, lost forever. Now our handbags were being confiscated as well. We were allowed to keep eyeglasses and toothbrushes and, while removing them, we managed to quickly and secretly stash documents, letters, and photographs into our coat pockets. Gone for good were the sewing kits, towels, washcloths, soap. Also lost were my Bible and my small first edition of *Robinson Crusoe,* the loyal companion of many years. To him I owed some of the skills a person needs to tenaciously carve an existence out of nothing. He taught me how to preserve a positive balance in life, even though abandoned by fate, and helped me learn how to be grateful for the good God grants us in spite of everything.

We were counted outside the archway: 122 women out of 260 new arrivals. The gate was opened, but only as long as needed to march us through, and then its iron bars slammed shut behind us. According to the markings on the wooden barracks and the carts, we were now in the women's concentration camp.

The first order of business led us to the washhouse, the "sauna," where the actual processing began. We undressed, had our hair cut—

New women prisoners selected for work march toward the camp after having their heads shaved, being deloused, disinfected, and registered, given camp clothing, and in most cases being tattooed with their prison numbers. Yad Vasham Photo Archives; National Archives.

no, actually our heads were shaved to stubble; then came the showers and finally the tattoos.[18] This was where they confiscated the very last vestiges of our belongings; nothing remained, none of our clothes or underwear, no soap, no towel, no needle, and no utensils, not even a spoon; no written document that could have identified us, no picture, no written message from a loved one. Our past was cut off, erased. Only our name reminded us of it, but that, too, was to disappear along with everything else connected with it. We were put in prisoner garb with no underwear, only a thin chemise. We were issued brownish-yellow fatigues to distinguish us from the Poles, who wore blue-and-grey-striped overalls. We were given wooden shoes with shreds of Jewish prayer shawls (*talles*) as foot-wrappings. Then we got our numbers, burned into the left forearm and sewn onto our clothes within a triangular badge that identified each prisoner by color.[19] We were cut off from the whole world out there, uprooted from our homeland, torn from our families, a mere number, of significance only for bookkeepers. Nothing remained but naked existence—and for most of us not even that for very long—and the thoughts in our hearts. Of those even the SS couldn't rob us, and they are the only thing we managed to salvage.

The Gypsy Camp*

THREE WOMEN PHYSICIANS out of our transport were selected immediately upon arrival because we were needed in the Gypsy camp in

---

* Europe's Gypsies fell under the Race Laws of 1935 promulgated at Nuremberg. They ranked below Jews on the ladder of life considered "unworthy to be lived." Both Jews and Gypsies were in official language "parasites."

Birkenau.[20] For the time being, however, this distinction didn't spare us from being assigned the task of carrying stones. Our timid objection of having special status as physicians only earned us a few eardrum-splitting slaps. It was two days later, on May 21st, that we were officially assigned to our new duties. In the dressing room we were issued underwear, shoes, a nice uniform, and a snowy-white smock. In addition, and totally superfluously given the situation, each of us also received a second outfit to alternate with the first. Then we were brought to the infirmary to be introduced to the camp physician.

This infirmary was a small wooden barracks to the right of the entrance to the women's camp, where patients came for ambulatory care. We arrived just as the morning routines were ending and were led into a small room to wait for the camp doctor. The furnishings consisted of a single wooden table and a bench that ran along the wall, but the room itself was bright, well lit, and warm, with a wide window. After the excitement and the exhaustion of the past few days, we enjoyed the comfortable peace. The women helpers were friendly—it was the first time in the camp that anyone had greeted us politely; they chatted and interrogated us with the same curiosity with which old-timers everywhere receive the newcomer. One brought us some warm soup, asked about our backgrounds, about the journey, and above all about the conditions outside—about bombardments, the food supply, and the general morale in Germany as well as elsewhere in the occupied areas. They were only too willing to let themselves be infected by our optimistic prognosis that things couldn't continue for much longer. For our part, we took advantage of the conversation to learn about conditions in the camp, about this and that, about our duties as physicians, about the food, about the camp doctor. Finally we asked what the summons of the twenty right after they arrived meant and to what type of work they would be assigned. We asked this because the sister of one of us, a young thirty-year-old woman in her prime, had been among them. "They were singled out and sent directly to the gas."

All three of us were sitting on the bench. The helper was standing in front of us and spoke calmly, indifferently, in the same tone she had used a moment ago when describing her duties in the clinic and the distribution of the soup. We learned that the people who had been herded onto the trucks went directly to the crematorium, where they were gassed and then cremated. She went on to tell us how good the work in the outpatient room was, in the "Aryan" outpatient room, that is, where Jews were admitted on an individual basis and only in exceptional cases. She told us how efficient the gynecologist was, how difficult, if not impossible, it was to drum up any soap to wash the white smocks; the words rained down upon us incessantly. And yet, the room had suddenly turned icy cold; we shivered down to the marrow of our bones, and our hands were clammy with sweat. I had to strain to keep my teeth from chattering audibly. The colleague next to me trembled all over, but managed to remain outwardly calm while she chatted about outpatient care.

A few hours later the camp physician appeared.[21] He received us in a collegial manner, almost graciously, and seemed, so we thought, to be a very nice man. He minced no words in telling us about the diseases rampant in the Gypsy camp, outlined our daily duties, and generously promised us the necessary instruments and pertinent technical literature. Apart from an epidemic of typhus in the Gypsy camp, everything sounded very auspicious. He dismissed us with good instructions, and we set out for the Gypsy camp. We didn't get any farther than the gate of the women's camp, however, the same one we had come through two days earlier, because we weren't allowed to leave the camp alone and had to wait for an SS escort. Near the gate but still inside the compound stood a woman with a sign around her neck: "I stole a piece of bread and must stand for three days as punishment." She was still standing there, and just as motionless, when a female SS guard with two huge, snappish dogs came to collect us a good hour later. We were marched briskly through the gate and then around the camp along the high barbed-wire fence, which was punctuated by ubiquitous watchtowers and frequently interrupted by huge entrance gates similar to the ones leading to the women's compound; a good twenty minutes later we approached the Gypsy camp. Its entrance, like all others, was flanked by a guardhouse. Our numbers were recorded, the gate was opened, again for only as long as it took to run through, and immediately bolted behind us. We were now in the Gypsy camp.

Still accompanied by the guard and her dogs, we walked along the main street of the camp, a bumpy dirt road pitted with holes full of stagnant water covered with a dull greyish-green film. The road led through the middle of the camp and was lined on both sides with closely situated rows of barracks called "blocks." As we trotted along that evening after roll call, the street was full of people—men, women, and many children wandering about in motley garments and colorful scarves, all laughing, chatting, talking loudly and animatedly among themselves. At the sight of the guard they immediately froze and fell silent, watched us suspiciously, and only gradually resumed their former activities. If the many dark-skinned people and the screaming colors of the wild and haphazardly combined garments hadn't lent the whole scene such an exotic atmosphere, we might have thought it was the eve of a village festival. The guard hastened us along, pushing us through the crowds almost to the end of the street to block 30, the penultimate of the sixteen barracks buildings on each side. There she dropped us off, and the camp as well as the block elder, both prominent personalities in the camp, received us.

The camp elder* welcomed us newcomers warmly and was instantly ready to help. She regretted the fact that there was no closet, no drawer, not even a wooden shelf at our disposal to store our things. Obviously looking out for our interests, she offered to take all the equipment as well as everything else we had with us, with the exception of what we were wearing at the moment, into her keeping. This she did immediately and very insistently.

The block elder,** a tightrope artist by profession, was a slim Gypsy with a very symmetrical, oval face, brown skin, and pitch-black, velvety hair. In her white turban, which was tied in a diamond-shaped knot at the front, she looked like an Indian snake-dancer out of some feature film. She received us with a lukewarm and indifferent air and didn't have much time for us. Her little room, as foreign as her appearance, draped with a motley collection of dirty rags and equipped with a wide pallet that served alternately as a bed and a canteen table for the block's rations—and continued to do so even after she contracted typhus—never lacked male company. She reluc-

---

* The German *Lagerälteste* signified a camp supervisor chosen from among the female prisoners and responsible for order on all camp premises.

** The German *Blockälteste* signified a barracks supervisor chosen from among the female prisoners and responsible for order in the barracks and its environs during roll calls, food distribution, "selections," and other rituals of camp life.

other barracks, it was nothing more than an unconverted former horse stable. It had no windows, and the scant light it did admit entered through a narrow ribbon of glass that ran beneath the roof rafters. The wind blew with all its fury through the broad crevices in the wooden walls; cold and heat penetrated unobstructed, and the rain streamed through the holes and cracks in the inadequately tarred roof, soaking the dirt floor as well as the patients' bunks. Both longitudinal walls of the block were lined with as many "beds" as could be crammed in, three-tiered wooden bunks with boards that didn't fit and constantly shifted around in every direction. On top of these lay the torn and paltry straw mattresses and threadbare, tattered blankets that passed for the patients' sleeping arrangements.

The block's remaining inventory consisted of two wooden tables and a stove, a broad-ledged brick construction with two large openings front and back; this stove ran along the length of the block. The doctors sat on it, as did also the clerks when they worked at their tables composing the meticulous medical reports and fever curves. Those patients who could still crawl out of bed also crouched on top of it, clothed in shirts that were much too short or in the shreds of what had previously been some sort of garment. This stove was also the reception area for new patients brought in from the camp; here they deposited their filthy and lice-infested possessions, and, because of the lack of a proper table, it was here that we also examined them. When it came time to dole out the food, bowls of soup were placed on this stove and bread was cut on its unwashed, uncovered stones. The stove was the focal point of every activity; people climbed over it with their dirty belongings whenever they wanted to get from one side of the block to the other. Injections were given and abscesses lanced; in unguarded moments the Gypsy aides practiced the foxtrot

Mulo, Mulo

This photograph, taken January 27, 1945, shows women resting on bunks shortly after being liberated from Auschwitz-Birkenau. The Nazis had crammed hundred of prisoners into this barracks, originally designed to house fifty-two horses. Central Armed Forces Museum, Moscow, courtesy of the U.S. Holocaust Memorial Museum.

or a belly dance there, accompanied by the newest hit. We ate there, "cooked" there, washed there with the little water we had—contaminated, filthy brown water that stained everything yellow because of its iron content.

Frequently enough, we even slept on top of this stove. After all, lying on hard stones was still better than sleeping in the overcrowded bunks. Eight hundred to a thousand or more persons in one single barracks block was the rule. Emaciated, feverish individuals would lie crammed in their berths, next to, on top of, beneath each other, ten to a space that ordinarily would have sufficed for two or four people at the most. It might have been a little more bearable way up top, where the more agile patients who were still able to climb were bedded, if only the rain hadn't so soaked their blankets and straw mattresses that they never dried out and the water dripped down to the middle tiers. Below, where the seriously sick who no longer had the strength to sit up or crawl out of bed to attend to their business were berthed, was a mire of feces- and urine-drenched blankets. The dying writhed among the dead, emitting a dull, extended moan that sounded like the cry of an animal perishing in the forest primeval.

We had a number of nurses' aides. Many of them were Gypsies—former artists, well-formed, good-looking women—who had absolutely no interest in the sick. Their job involved little more than doling out the rations (always making sure they took good care of themselves while doing so). They were also supposed to take temperatures, although many of them were unable to read or write. They displayed a childlike joy in dresses and baubles, were constantly trading the garments they had been allowed to keep, and changed their clothes a number of times a day. What had previously served as a costume was not all that suited for their new occupation. I can still see Resi with her dark curls and flashing eyes prancing back and forth in a black silk skirt and a waist-length tunic of silver brocade with wide, voluminous, long-flowing sleeves—a jewel from her show-booth days. One day, when the SS guards swept through the block on patrol, she hastily grabbed two overflowing chamber pots and carried them away. With every step her swinging sleeves sank deeper and deeper into the slosh.

The doctors, good and bad, decent and indecent, experienced

practitioners and bloody charlatans with no training whatsoever, were powerless.[22] They had hundreds of patients to care for and were required to fill out detailed case reports for each one of them. These reports had to be faultless and updated every three days, a full-time job in itself. At the same time and at the risk of "twenty-five strokes of the oxtail," they also had to guarantee the accuracy of the ever-changing head count. This was rarely exact in the excessively over-crowded and unoverseeable blocks, where twenty to thirty patients were taken in each day and no fewer died, where the dying in their agony crept into their straw sack or, unnoticed, perished behind a beam. The patients were counted again and again and the results compared, and as soon as we were done, we repeated the whole process again because more had died in the meantime.

Once I made five full counts, but the total never came out right. One patient was always missing, and there was never an answer when her number was called. Maybe she had died and her body been tossed on the hearse before she could be counted or deleted from the list. I was beside myself: "twenty-five"—I knew I wouldn't survive. Only strong men lived through that. In my desperation I sent someone to the block where the patient's husband was being held. Maybe she had secretly gone back to him. With measured steps her husband came over: a handsome man with a long white beard and white turban. He listened to my plight and began to whistle a short, melodic strain. A few seconds later an ugly old Gypsy woman threw herself around his neck. She'd been hiding in a straw mattress and hadn't stirred. I was so relieved I almost embraced her husband as well.

With all of this going on, there wasn't much time left for treat-ment, not that the camp direction seemed to consider treatment necessary, in any case. Medications were scarce—two camphor ampoules and one bottle of *digitalis infus** were to last approximately one week. The only thing we did have in any quantity was *bolus alba,*** not in boxes or bags but by the sackful. Bolus, this white powder, was our panacea; it was given internally for diarrhea, dabbed on mucous membranes in cases of stomatitis, and sprinkled over inflammations of the skin. The bunks and the walls were also painted with a thick paste of the stuff so that they shone white against all our misery.

The only thing the doctors could do for their patients, emaciated, skeletal, or swollen with the edema of starvation and wallowing in feverish deliriums as they were, was to comfort and encourage them. It didn't make them any better: they still died like flies. And again and again, rising up between the death rattles of the dying and the drawn-out moans of the critically ill was the Gypsy call: "*Mulo, mulo* [a corpse, a corpse]."

The bodies were pulled out of the bunks and dragged just as they were—filthy and feces-encrusted—along the muddy corridor between the bunks and the stove toward the back of the block, where they were tossed into a corner. There they remained until the corpse commando came in the evening to remove the towering heaps. No pleas, no orders could bring the aides to the point of treating these cadavers with any degree of dignity. When life doesn't mean anything anymore, respect for the dead doesn't either.

---

* Latin for the heart stimulant prepared by steeping dried foxglove leaves in water to make it infusible.

** Latin for any mass of medicinal material, usually in pill form but capable of being powdered by crushing.

Mulo, mulo, a corpse, a corpse; nothing but corpses. Twenty, thirty a day; in one block, in every block.

Sunday in the Camp

ONE DAY a general sense of excitement pervaded the Gypsy camp, for a special performance had been conceived to celebrate Sunday. The big open space between the washroom and the kindergarten was to serve as an open-air stage. As one would expect in a children's playground, there were swings and all sorts of gymnastic equipment, including rings, bars, and a wooden fence without barbed wire. The performance began at 5 P.M.; the whole camp, some sixteen thousand people in the Gypsy camp alone, had gathered together. The audience crowded against the perimeter of this wooden fence; the performers stood in a semicircle in the area next to the block, ready to go. In front of them was an improvised podium where they played the music—five Gypsies with violins (the Gypsies had kept their musical instruments, along with all the rest of their belongings) and another with an accordion and a wooden leg. They abandoned themselves completely to the lilting, erotic melodies with their undertone of yearning and despair, those beguiling airs that reflect how these people live and love, as free and unbounded and instinctual as the animals in the wild, all the while still managing to betray a last dark echo of their original homeland in India. The gymnasts began to swing and sway to the rhythm; they piled themselves into high pyramids, spun in circles, and rolled like balls, no longer prisoners but once again pure and passionate performers. Nothing was lacking, not even the clown—that genuinely theatrical figure that hides its true human face behind a made-up mask and painted-on grimace.

The audience gave an even better performance: the crowd along the fence shouted their approval, they booed, they sang, and they danced along with the music. A Gypsy audience is a sight in itself; it participates not with applause but with its whole body, with every muscle. The children were already being taught how to perform and dance, and the first stroke of the violin bow or the squeeze of the accordion set even the tiniest tot in motion. Arms, legs, heads, every body swirled about and every body jumped. A variety show in the camp, on both sides of the fence: Gypsy Sunday!

Suddenly there's a piercing whistle, a commando,* and the show breaks off in the middle. "Block confinement" is the order, which means that everyone has to return to the blocks immediately. In no time the crowds are driven back to their barracks, not to the strains of music but to the blows of clubs and sticks. The play space, as well as the main street, is deserted in no time.

We've hardly returned to our block before the doors are bolted shut behind us. No one is allowed to go near the door or even to look through a crack. An anxious silence engulfs the entire block. The sick cease their moaning, the healthy crawl quickly into their bunks without even taking the time to gulp down their rations in the usual manner. Newcomers though we are, we, too, sense the atmosphere of doom. Sleep is out of the question. We lie cowering on our straw mattresses and press together as closely as possible. Now and then, a

---

* The German *kommando* signified a temporary work crew. There were at any given time more than three hundred within Auschwitz, composed of as few as fifty or as many as twelve hundred workers each. A few smaller permanent *kommandos* engaged in light work such as registration. Belonging to one of these improved chances for survival.

hushed whisper; otherwise, an uncanny silence reigns supreme in the block, which on other days is reminiscent of a monkey cage with all its shrieking. Hours pass and it gradually grows dark. Then the automobiles approach. The reflection of headlights on the wall tells us that one is turning toward our block. We hear the motor stop. The doors are thrown open. The SS appear. Names and numbers are called out and blinding flashlights, searching for these numbers, scan the arms of every patient and every aide. We don't dare breathe anymore, don't dare even turn our heads. Who's next? When will our number be called? Whether it's half an hour or minutes or even only seconds before the outside gate is shut again and the car puffs and snorts away, we have no idea.

On this particular night twenty-five hundred Czech Gypsies were sent to the gas chambers. It was our second Sunday in the camp, the 30th of May, 1943.[23] From then on, we knew that all laughter and all playacting in the camp meant only one thing: it was only a prelude.

Hunger

WE DIDN'T HAVE to wait very long for our own case of typhus. It struck in June. Once the fever had abated, like the other patients I was isolated in the quarantine block for three weeks before being permitted to resume my duties. It was stifling hot in these blocks, with the setting sun beating down on them and the cracks and narrow openings beneath the roof beams admitting hardly a breath of air when the weather was calm. I was lying by a hole in a corner on the top bunk right beneath the roof. Through this opening I could just make out a speck of sky and, through the glass strip opposite me, even a few tree tops, and way out, through the open door, a tiny stretch of yellow speckled meadow. The surrounding bunks were all crawling with naked Gypsy women, who passed the time telling each other fantastic stories about their former wealth, by trading things and exchanging recipes, the inexhaustible topic of conversation among starving people. They babbled in a mishmash of all languages, punctuated with their own Gypsy idiom, which sounded harsh and piercing to the ear. With the distant green in the background and the brown bodies lying listlessly about amidst incessant chatter, and with a squint of the eye, one could almost conjure up the illusion of being on a beach. Sometimes, my fever-weary head and blurry thoughts let me doze through hours on end; when that happened, time and space would dissolve and fear and horror melt away, and in the midst of all this noise an enormous peace would engulf me as if I were one with the universe and the natural world outside.

Of course, among other things lacking in our pseudo summer outings in the camp was food. Like a lot of other infectious diseases, typhus has the diabolical side effect of increasing one's appetite during convalescence, a totally gratuitous sensation in light of the fact that our daily rations consisted exclusively of a pint of camp soup and half a pound of bread with less than an ounce of margarine or sausage; at other times the daily regimen consisted of a quarter loaf of white bread and a pint of watery porridge. It has been shown that a diet like this, without potatoes, without between-meal snacks, without all the little things one normally and unconsciously pops into one's mouth during the course of the day, will lead to starvation in six months.

One Sunday, the 25th of July, misfortune struck us all when they failed to deliver the soup. No one had any bread left, since we usually gobbled it down whole, with an atavistic resemblance to a boa constrictor, as soon as it was distributed every morning. Even so, such manners didn't produce the desired effect of feeling full. No soup meant a long day with nothing to eat. Whoever has known true starvation knows that hunger is not merely an autonomic animalistic sensation in the stomach, but a nerve-shattering pain, an attack on the whole personality. Hunger makes a person vicious and undermines her character. Many of the things the prisoners did, things that rightly seem outrageous and monstrous to the outsider, become understandable and to a certain extent excusable when seen from the perspective of starvation. Worn down like this by hunger and no longer in control of myself, I yearned for, I craved something to eat. And then, when right before my eyes, two non-Jewish Polish aides who had permission to travel started to smear their boots with margarine, starvation made me howl and sob like a child.

That same evening a sprightly young Gypsy girl from the Rhineland came to visit. She'd been in the camp since March and told me how in those days she had had to stand at roll call for hours on end in the freezing snow; she told me about all the food she had brought with her from home and how the prisoners in the neighboring block had suffered from starvation. Bread and soup were doled out sporadically and then only sparingly. And when the worst-off mustered their last ounce of energy to pounce on the garbage and the potato peels in the snow or to rummage around in the trash cans, they were mercilessly beaten off and, as punishment, deprived of their rations. Heaps of people, fifty, sixty in a single block, starved or beaten to death, surrounded the barracks blocks every day. I was profoundly ashamed of myself. There were always others who suffered much more than I did and they alone could set the standard. I resolved never again to cry because of hunger, and I kept my promise to the end, even later when but a hair separated me from starving to death.

This May 1944 photograph depicts roll call for new women prisoners at Auschwitz-Birkenau. These women have not yet been given camp clothing. Yad Vasham Photo Archives.

The next morning, July 26, 1943, we heard that the British and the Americans had landed in Italy.[24] We were a millimeter closer to freedom.

Roll Call

ROLL CALL in the concentration camp was the horror of the day. It was held to determine and to keep a continuous record of the precise "stand," that is, the precise number of prisoners. If one considers how large the individual camps in Birkenau were—the women's concentration camp alone had an average of twenty-five to thirty-five thousand inmates, the other ancillary camps between ten and twenty thousand; if one considers that part of the SS system of maintaining constant unrest was the daily shifting of prisoners from one section of the camp to another; if one then takes into further consideration the many hundreds of prisoners who collapsed and dropped dead at or on the way to work or in a hidden corner of their block, then one will have some idea of what it took to make sure the actual roll call agreed with the expected total and to what extremes the main offices, the block clerks, and everyone else who was responsible for the count, including the doctors, had to go; every missing person meant severe punishments for all of us. Not only the number of the living but that of the dead, as well, had to match. No one could be left unaccounted for. That meant that every death had to be reported precisely, along with the victim's number; this information had to be entered and the name deleted from the books in the office well before roll call. If you were not dead, you had to appear at roll call, notwithstanding a fever of 104, diarrhea, or cardiac weakness. This included everyone, even people thinner than sticks, with frozen hands and feet.

Twice a day we stood at roll call, in the dark hours before dawn prior to marching off to work (in the summer we got up at 3 A.M. and in the winter at 4) and again in the evening after work. Each time, the roll call lasted one to two hours, frequently much longer. Should the supervisors be in a bad mood, should there be an instance of so-called punishment, or should the count not match, roll call could drag on indefinitely.[25]

Woe betide us if one should be missing, be it because—rarely enough—she had managed to escape, be it because a transfer to a different section of the camp had been overlooked, an inmate had been commandeered to work or sent to a transport and not been checked off, or perhaps someone, ignoring the roll call altogether, had perished unseen in some far-off corner and escaped our attention. Anything of the sort sufficed to send a whole section of the camp into total confusion. We were counted again and again, often by calling out every single number, and the prisoners had to stand, not only hours on end, but days, nights. A roll call that lasted a day and a night without interruption was nothing unusual, and many prisoners have stood twenty-four and forty-eight hours in the broiling sun, in pouring rain, in frigid, subzero weather with howling winds—with total disregard, of course, for the fact that their clothes were less than adequate. They stood in threadbare shreds of garments, in wooden clogs or worn-out and split remnants of what once had been leather shoes, their hands wrapped in a few rags. And they stood still, for they were not allowed to move. They stood with the wet and clammy tatters clinging to their bodies, with nothing in their stomachs, and were forbidden to excuse themselves when bouts of diarrhea caused the excrement to stream out like a waterfall. Furtively and inconspicuously they pressed up against one another to keep warm, and thus they supported their comrades when they began to reel. If you fell, you remained where you landed; with any luck you were spared a beating. As a rule you were usually treated to beatings, whippings, and pistol lashings until you got back on your feet. If you collapsed a second time, the whole procedure was repeated until you never got up again.

This is not to say that such abuse was limited to roll call; it was

equally distributed between roll call and work detail and wasn't unknown during the brief night hours in the blocks, either. The only
difference was that, at roll call, you were there and had to watch it all
(always supposing you weren't the object). To stand by, powerless
and unable to help, to have to watch while another person is being
tortured, is one of the worst experiences of this life. I still believe that
today. This having to stand by, totally self-controlled, with clenched
teeth and secretly clenched fists, forced to let anything happen while
not being able to help a friend in distress, was the rule in Auschwitz,
and roll call its perfidious name.

The story of the father who was beaten to death before the very
eyes of his son was repeated in Auschwitz with every possible variation. In January of 1945 a woman, swollen with the edema of starvation, was brought to my station from the weaving mill; her body was
black and blue all over. During roll call the whole block had to kneel
in the snow because the prisoners in the mill had failed to make their
quota by a few meters. My patient pleaded for mercy for her fever-
stricken daughter. In response, the daughter was thrown to the
ground, pummeled with fists, and trampled with heavy boots; the
mother was severely abused as well.

Repelled by such horrors, many people will choose to ignore these
terrible testimonies simply to preserve their inner peace; I know, because I used to do the same thing myself. Others, who refuse to believe that the reality of Auschwitz exceeded all human imagination,
will dismiss these reports as propagandistic fantasy.[26] This and this
alone has led me to whatever positive attitude I have about my im-
prisonment in the concentration camp. If such things really do happen on this earth, you have to witness them with your own eyes
because no one will believe it otherwise or they will prefer, out of

laziness or a desire not to get involved, to respond with indifference. And yet, in the end, knowledge of the deepest abysses of the human psyche is an absolute, vital necessity, for the path out of the lowest depths can only lead upwards.

There is another perverse advantage to having experienced these things personally; not having done so leaves people in ignorance as to just how much one human being can bear. The prisoners in concentration camps stood roll call day and night, on empty stomachs, in foul and frigid weather, and they endured; as a rule they weren't defeated by it as long as gratuitous brutality didn't put an end to them. They stood without complaining, without crying, without ducking, and without wincing, full of calm and dignity, as if it were a matter of course. Roll call was not only the horror of the day; it was also a revelation as to how human beings can rise above themselves.

Typhus

ON THAT FIRST DAY the camp physician told us we would find two unusual diseases plaguing the Gypsy camp, a plethora of noma (gangrenous mouth ulcers), avitaminosis (extraordinarily rare in central Europe), and a rampant typhus epidemic. The number of typhus cases was six hundred when we arrived in this small part of the camp, and it burgeoned to about one thousand in July and August. Typhus is passed on by lice—by bites and by microscopic particles of lice excrement floating in the air. There was good reason to plaster warning signs all over the camp, whose bold letters and graphic illustrations proclaimed: ONE SINGLE LOUSE MEANS DEATH! Unfortunately, the lice didn't take sufficient notice of these signs; the blocks were crawling with them even more densely than with people, which was possible only because lice are smaller than people. As mentioned above, we three newcomers were immediately infected by our lice-infested block-mates.

As a complication to her typhus, one of my colleagues contracted an inflammation of the brain, so gruesome in itself that I still shudder to think of it. In her horrible distress she tossed about like a *perpetuum mobile;** shamelessly exposing her nakedness, she threw off all blankets and pillows and twisted her emaciated body in snake-like coils all over the bunk, her arms circling in their sockets. She was no longer a person, but an encephalated animal. She sobbed incessantly, screamed herself hoarse, and stammered unfinished words in incoherent passages of prayer. She calmed down just before she died, reduced to a mere skeleton with distorted features.

My second companion contracted abdominal typhus along with her fever, complete with diarrhea and phlebitis. With legs swollen to the knee, she was unable to get to the latrine quickly enough. She was mocked not only by the Gypsy aides but also by our non-Jewish male colleague, who made fun of her with derisive verses, and she was beaten half to death. In the end she lay in her own excrement near the latrine, craving potatoes and vitamins that no one could bring her, until she, too, perished miserably.

The next to go was a male colleague from Zagreb. Not long before, the SS had tossed him beneath a pile of corpses on the hearse, and this punishment had just about suffocated him. Quite by accident an

---

* Latin for the perpetual motion of a machine that in theory lost no energy from friction or other dissipation, hence capable of operation without energy applied from without. This expression could be applied broadly to the overworked, starved, and diseased inmates.

earlier acquaintance recognized and rescued the man, thus saving him from "going up the chimney"* alive. Soon after this, however, he fell victim to typhus, and a cardiac arrest put an end to his suffering.

Many others followed, and then came the turn of one of the doctors, a renowned scientist in his own right. As the situation in his homeland became more and more precarious, some of his friends urged him to leave the country. He refused to go on the grounds that he found any covert action reprehensible. Thus, he came to Auschwitz with the Norwegian transport, a few of whose men were sent to the camp but all of whose women were sent indiscriminately to the gas chambers.[27] He never forgave himself for leading his wife to her death and was unable to comprehend the fact that Auschwitz, too, was a forum in which Providence itself determined the actors as well as the extras.

In September of 1943 this doctor was transferred to the isolation barracks with a high fever. He had contracted what was known as an "elegant" case of typhus, one that doesn't destroy the brain cells and doesn't involve diarrhea. He lay there in quarantine with the stoic calm of a person awaiting death with equanimity. At the same time he also experienced that doubling of the self peculiar to many forms of this disease: the patient is completely oriented to reality while simultaneously living in a dream world that lacks nothing of the clarity of actual being. I remember observing every single detail in the Gypsy block during my bout with the fever while at the same time sojourning in the Engadin behind Sils-Maria in the Malojan Heights,

---

* The common camp phrase for the gassing and cremation of biologically exhausted or otherwise disabled prisoners.

with the sun playing over Segantini's grave* and myself gazing out onto the bluish-pink fields of the Bergell Valley. In much the same way, this man wandered back and forth between the typhus barracks in Birkenau and the medical conferences in Europe. With a raging fever of 104 degrees, he discussed the scientific problems of tuberculosis in his native language, carefully weighing, evaluating, and rejecting every consideration in turn; a few minutes later he could be found evaluating his own medical condition in fluent German. And yet, with all this intellectual agility, his typhus was a malignant case. His heart was not functioning adequately and his pulse was weak. Bad days were followed by worse nights.

I'll never forget this vigil: The weather was miserable, with a storm howling around the blocks and penetrating through the ubiquitous cracks in the walls straight to the marrow of our bones. Rain poured down in buckets and streamed through the cracks and holes in the roof onto the dirt floor below. Dampness insinuated itself through our wet clothing, the only clothes we had, and into every pore; our shoes squished with water and stuck to our feet. And there lay that man with irregular pulse, shallow breathing, and blue lips in a barracks where untold numbers of people died of typhus every day.

On one of those nights—it was the 29th of September and the Jewish New Year—I rebelled against God: What's it all for? Why another year? All my friends in the camp had died; it seemed the best were always the first to go. There was no hope left for any of us. What

---

* Giovanni Segantini (1858–1899), Italian landscape painter who settled in the Engadin region of Switzerland in 1894, hence the exact geographical references. In her hallucinatory state Dr. Adelsberger perhaps recalled his triptych "Life, Nature, and Death."

was the use of all this grief and all this despair? What was the purpose of this hell we were living in if no one survived to open the book someday and tell the story of the victims of Auschwitz?[28]

The crisis came five days later. The patient's fever abated and he abandoned himself to the healthy sleep of convalescence. After weeks on end, we could finally leave him unattended. I stood behind the block and gazed at the chimneys; the sun had broken through again and was hanging like a red cannonball in the evening sky. Suddenly I was overwhelmed by the thought that, despite it all, life is still stronger than death. Some day a new life would arise, phoenixlike, from the ashes of the dead of Auschwitz.

• PART THREE •

Candy for the Little Ones

THE BLOCK USED for the children's infirmary in the Gypsy camp was not much different from those the adults lived in, but the privation these youngsters endured was all the more heartrending, perhaps because their faces had lost all signs of childhood and their hollow eyes peered out through the jaded expressions of old age. Even the wildest imagination of a Holbein* or a Rethel** would have failed to capture the emaciated body and deathlike mask that suffering and starvation had created in Birkenau.

Like the adults, these children were no more than skin and bones, with no muscles and no body fat. Their transparent, parchmentlike skin was chafed and rubbed sore over the sharp angles of their bones and erupted in festering wounds. Scabies covered their undernourished bodies from head to foot and sucked out their last ounce of strength. Their mouths were infested with malignant noma ulcers that riddled their lips and perforated their cheeks. In spite of all this, these children ate and drank, and some of them recovered temporarily and even seemed cured. For many others, starvation bloated their disintegrating bodies. They swelled to misshapen blobs, unable to move. Diarrhea, for weeks on end, dissolved the nonresistant body until, under the constant outflow of whatever substance it might have had, nothing was left.

---

* Presumably Hans Holbein the Younger (1497–1543). Born at Augsburg, he migrated to England in 1526 and became Court Painter to Henry VIII.

** Alfred Rethel (1816–1859) was born near Aachen but worked in Bavaria and Switzerland, primarily on historical frescoes.

Many of these children had had nothing to eat for so long that they no longer asked for food, but they all craved something to drink. Even those whose bodies seemed to have stored up much too much fluid begged incessantly for water. Thirst, unquenchable thirst, was one of the great torments of Birkenau. Water was forbidden because it was contaminated; the three buckets of coffee or tea, a lightly discolored beverage, were but a mockery of the thousand parched throats in the block. Hunger kills, but an unquenchable thirst drives you crazy. No cajoling, no threat could keep these children from drinking: they traded their last morsel of bread for a beaker of the contaminated water, and when they no longer had the strength to walk, they would crawl from their berths at night and secretly scramble on all fours beneath the bunks toward the pails of dirty wash water and gulp down the very last drop.

Hunger, thirst, cold, and pain gave these youngsters no peace, not even at night. Their moanings intensified like hurricanes and echoed through the block until, exhausted, they slackened off for a bit, only to rise to a new crescendo after a brief pause. Night after night the wails of these suffering creatures surged and ebbed like the waves of the sea, a never-ending symphony of human misery. If those who callously ignore human suffering could have spent but three nights in the children's block, where we had our sleeping quarters, many things might have been different. Or if they had even once witnessed the morning ablutions, had seen how the children were taken from their bunks along with their filthy blankets, how they were pulled out from under the rotten straw sacks crawling with maggots, how they lay on top of the cold tiles of the "stove" or on the dirt floor and were washed, still clinging to their blankets, and how the whole lot was dragged back to bed—wet, sick children wrapped up in the damp rags that passed for blankets.

And yet, and this was the wonder of it all, even these little ones had their pleasures and their happy moments. Starting in November, uncooked oatmeal with sugar was added to their starvation rations, a small little pile for each child. They stopped in their tracks as soon as they heard "Oatmeal!" and when the big blue enamel bowl with the dry flakes and the small white porcelain sugar pot were carried into the room, their eyes lit up and never let the bearers of their treasure out of sight for even a moment. A small amount was placed in the hollow of each little hand, and with total concentration they ate one flake after the other and carefully licked each and every finger.

There was only one thing these youngsters considered an even greater treat: the day the camp physician came to visit. They knew nothing of his business with the gas chambers and nothing of the fact that we trembled with every visit, for the slightest provocation put our lives and those of many others on the line. All they knew was the candy he brought in his bulging pockets. He handed it out one piece at a time, sometimes tossing it to them playfully and now and again pressing a piece into the hand of one too sick to move. He never had enough for all, but every child had his turn, if not today then tomorrow or the day after. The camp physician had only to appear for the little ones to beam with joy. One piece of candy, and they forgot the misery of their surroundings.

The children weren't the only ones; the adults did the same thing. A bowl of cold camp soup, two boiled potatoes, or a beaker of milk as a special treat kept their fear of starvation at bay and cheered them up for a while. Often enough, all that was needed was a gentle stroke, a comforting word, a tiny token of affection.

The Dentist

JUST WHY HE was in the concentration camp was never apparent, any more than whether he was an ethnic German[29] or a member of some other nationality. The only thing we knew for sure was that he was no Jew. Whether or not he had fought in the Spanish civil war, or on which side, was not to be discovered. Some even suspected that he had sought out the concentration camp (where he was not personally required to bear arms) as a peaceful oasis in a war-weary world, or as an El Dorado in a starving Europe. He certainly had no worries on that score, for he stuffed himself with the finest of delicacies and dictated his menu according to whim.

The majority of his patients were SS men, whom he provided with beautiful new teeth and genuine gold crowns in return for prompt and generous deliveries from the camp warehouses and the kitchen. He was also on good terms with the prisoners, particularly the Poles with "purchasing power."[30] He took no interest in what was going on in the camp. He was a very skilled technician. He used his primitive instruments to drill one's teeth to bits and pieces without splitting the jawbone. And he had an absolutely sure means of quieting his inferior patients: the first peep was met with two earsplitting whacks to the side of the head, with the result that the patient lost both sight and hearing and was rendered quite tractable. Even so, this dentist was not disliked. With the instincts of a master of the art of living, he sniffed out the slightest opportunity in the camp to wend his cheerful way between the rows of open graves.

His fearlessness—he was never really in danger—had a beneficial effect. He did not brag. He had lived through a lot. Once, while high in the mountains somewhere, he had clambered up inaccessible and unpassable terrain; on a steep cliff he suddenly found himself face to face with a huge bear. This dentist put an end to the beast with the strength of his bare hands. Poisonous adders, poised to attack, were hypnotized by his glance. He was all for bravura and gallantry, as when he ushered in each new day in his cozy cell with a breakfast of Hungarian goulash and Viennese dumplings, or celebrated the evening with "brandy," an indefinable mixture of wood alcohol, ether, and other anesthetizing ingredients. He could never understand why the Jews marched like obedient sheep to the crematoria out of consideration for the others whom the SS were holding hostage, nor could he comprehend the fact that they did so without putting up any resistance.[31] Deep down he was a good-natured man. He shared his wealth with many and saved some from starvation, including a whole group of beautiful Gypsy women, one after the other of whom found their way into his chamber. And he knew how to throw a party. On Christmas Eve he invited us into the fir-bedecked dental clinic, replete with multicolored burning candles, and offered us Berlin pancakes and Viennese apple strudel—us! who never had enough bread and water. He'd even managed to engage a Gypsy musician, who sang Christmas carols while accompanying himself on the zither.

This dentist was one of those people who managed to make themselves at home in the camp, who dominated through privilege, and who perhaps at times still look back on those days with melancholy if not downright yearning.

On Death

THE DISTINGUISHING MARK of the concentration camp at Auschwitz was selection. By that I mean the sorting-out of people who were relegated to the gas chambers and subsequent cremation. It applied almost exclusively to Jews and involved three categories of people, three "entries": those newly arrived in Auschwitz, prisoners from the camp, and sick people from the compound. The old, the weak, and those obviously sick and unable to work were automatically relegated to selection, including all children under fourteen together with their mothers or those who had taken them on or under their wing. It was never entirely clear why the Germans retained the Latinate expression in this instance, for they normally and fanatically expunged every foreign word from their language, only to replace it by all sorts of clumsy circumlocutions.[32] Perhaps this choice fell under the rubric of camouflage, by which means they sought to disguise their demonic activities. Later on, they even went so far as to enclose the courtyards of the crematoria with thick hedges of green boxwood bushes. This was to create the illusion that someone behind the hedge, comfortably resting on a lounge chair in his garden, wanted to retreat from the curious glances of passers-by.

Officially, of course, we knew nothing of the selection, even though the flames licked the heavens before our very eyes and we were almost asphyxiated by the stench and the smoke. The mere word was taboo in any dealings with the SS. If an outsider had overheard how we bargained and haggled over human life, weighing arguments about a particular prisoner's ability to work or discussing the scientific significance of a particular case, he might have thought he was overhearing a harmless medical conference. I know of only one single exception to this rule. Before the liquidation of the Theresienstadt family camp in Birkenau,[33] which only 21 out of 3,500 inmates survived, one of my colleagues begged the camp physician to spare the life of her father, a renowned orthopedist. He denied her request on the grounds that the gas chamber would be a gentle death for a seventy-year-old man.

There's no doubt that the game of hide-and-seek did succeed with a number of new arrivals in Auschwitz and that it did delude them as to the true intentions of the SS, at least in the beginning. Whether it continued to do so up to the very end will remain an eternal secret. We of the group of '43 were not the only ones with no notion of what was going on; even the Hungarians who arrived as late as the summer of 1944 were just as ignorant.[34] What we who were already in the midst of things found incomprehensible was the fact that they took what they had heard on English-language radio broadcasts about the Auschwitz concentration camp for mere atrocity propaganda. (That's why I shouldn't be surprised when some people still shrug their shoulders out of disbelief when they hear about the fate of the prisoners of Auschwitz and mumble something about Jewish horror stories.) On the other hand, unlike us, the Polish Jews were generally aware of the evil awaiting them upon their arrival, be it because centuries of persecution had instilled in them a particular sense for danger, or be it because the extermination camps of Auschwitz, Majdanek, and Lublin were located on their own soil.[35] Conversation in our camp centered around a small, twelve-year-old Polish boy who had repeatedly assured the camp physician on the train that he could work like a man and that nothing was too hard for him. He never let up, and until the very end he resisted, vainly, being relegated to the children's group.

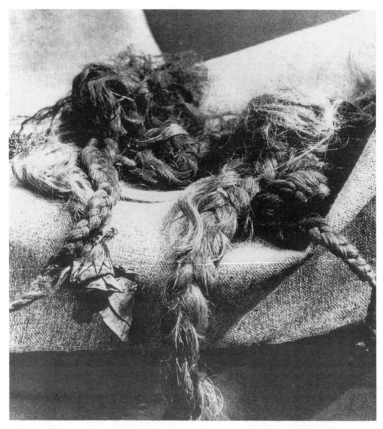

The Nazis exploited their victims for economic benefits beyond slave labor. Here we see the hair of women murdered at Auschwitz stored in a warehouse. Firms such as Alex Zink paid up to 50 pfennigs per kilogram for this hair. National Museum of Auschwitz-Birkenau, Oświęcim, Poland, courtesy of the U.S. Holocaust Memorial Museum.

On Death

No furtive attempts had any effect in the camp itself or in its compounds. The mechanism of selection was too firmly established, and
everyone knew its every detail. The camp physician commandeered
one or more blocks and ordered the naked prisoners to pass by in
single file. He then chose those who, because of weakness or under-
nourishment, the edema of starvation, or because of scabies or sun-
burn—there were reasons enough—were to go to the gas. The identification numbers of these unfortunates were recorded on the spot
and they were immediately transferred to the selection block, where
they waited for death, often without food and fully aware of their
fate. (Sometimes the political wing passed the numbers on directly,
without benefit of selection.) A few days or maybe a week later the
inevitable "block confinement" was announced. One heard the approach of automobiles, and if one were near enough, the screams of
people being beaten, accompanied by the fury of SS commands and
the barking of dogs; an hour or two later the chimneys were glowing.

The problem for us in Auschwitz was not whether selection, but
when and how. No Jewish prisoner reckoned on ever leaving Auschwitz alive. Not only did we live physically in the shadow of the chimneys but mentally as well. The chimney was the alpha and omega of
all conversation. It was spread on dry bread at breakfast and dished
up as dessert after every meal.

Death was as close and familiar to us as the landscape in which we
were born and raised. We saw him waiting implacably by the crematorium; and he took on many different shapes, not kindly ones with
friendly hands that stroked with affection, but forms with cruel features, with torment and torture, his arms covered with blood. Even
so, people, whose only desire was to live and not because they were
tired of fighting, calmly shook his hand and followed his nod without

hesitation, almost with a smile. They surrendered themselves to him because he was always with us and was one of us, like the sun and the light of day, like the moon and the stars in the night, like the very air we breathed. Of course, mothers grieved and lamented that they would never see their children again, and now and again someone begged for his or her life, like little Toes, the nineteen-year-old Dutch girl who wept in the selection block and implored: "Please help me; I'm young and I want to live." But these were very few. Many demonstrated a strength in dying that no Song of Songs could ever immortalize. Siblings parted from one another not with wailing but with dignity and courage; mothers, already in death's grip, comforted the children they were leaving behind; friends bade farewell with gratitude and affection. The story of the Belgian woman Mala, which is yet to be told, belongs here, as well as that of the Friday evening in January 1944. During those days the selections in Auschwitz were tripping over each other, and Birkenau was "cleansed" of Jews to within a tiny fraction of their previous numbers. Every evening had its block confinement. It got dark early and we were standing in our sealed-off block near the back door, peering through the cracks at the crematoria, one of which was no more than fifty meters away. It was the usual scene: trucks drove up, then stopped; the SS shouted commands, people were unloaded—just like always. And then, suddenly, out of the throats of hundreds of people as if from one, rhythmically and harmonically in the dark night, rose up the tones of *Schmah Israel*, "Hear, O Israel!"* This affirmation of faith echoed far

---

* More commonly "Shema Yisrael," the confession of faith in the unity of God found in Deuteronomy 6:4 and other passages of the Pentateuch. The prayer traditionally was recited for dying Jews, especially Jews suffering persecution and martyrdom.

and wide beneath the open skies, a hymn to God before the open portals of the death chambers. Hardened as we were by our life in the camp, we were hard pressed to stifle a sob and hardly managed to hold back our tears. One of my friends pulled herself together and hissed, "Shit. The soup's getting cold."

Why?

A FEW DAYS LATER we were standing at the window of the newly built laboratory that looked out on three crematoria. We were talking about various medical topics, about the body's ability to ward off infections and the digestive processes during starvation, for the SS camp physician had decided to introduce a series of lectures; between selections he wanted to hear something about diarrhea in the camp. We had already discussed these and other medical and nonmedical problems as well; it actually helped us forget the hunger and the horror of the inferno for a few hours. But today, in the blinding light of the insatiable flames—today we found it difficult to concentrate on the manifestations of eating disorders. Conversation lagged and soon died out altogether. We stared at the chimneys. "Why?" asked the comrade who was sure that this time his sister was one of the crowd over there. "Why is this happening to us? Are our shortcomings so egregious? We've gone our way, taken pains to be fair, and tried to help others. We haven't killed anyone and haven't committed any crime. And even for a murderer this punishment would be more than cruel. Why us, why?"

How often had we all asked ourselves the same question, during a moment of quiet reflection before falling asleep and again in the morning when we were rudely awakened, every moment of the day and during long night vigils. "Perhaps we've been too rigid and too hard and have to become more forgiving," I volunteered hesitantly. This kindly and good-natured man took offense at my answer. He had lost nine members of his family in Auschwitz.

Kohinoor*

THIS NEXT BRIEF EPISODE probably took place in March of 1944. Back then, the barracks within the compound of the Gypsy camp would have seemed quite presentable to the casual observer.[36] The walls and roofs gleamed in their whitewash; down below, a wainscoting had been added and treated with oil paint, something that was just about unobtainable in Germany by then and for which the prisoners in Birkenau paid dearly with their rations. The bunks were painted white and sported bleached sheets over the naked, emaciated bodies languishing on their rotten straw mattresses. And where once the bread rations for a full day were traded for a handful of water, several barracks even made a show of the mechanical apparatus needed for running water and flush toilets (for which amenities, however, the necessary drainage and sewerage arrangements were never installed). Flower vases graced the tables, and the walls of the children's blocks were decorated with familiar characters from kindergarten days: Little Red Riding Hood, Snow White and the Seven Dwarfs—so that, though the stomach may be empty, at least the imagination wasn't starving, and people were supposed to notice that even in Concentration Camp Auschwitz they knew something about fairy tales (something, by the way, that even the children didn't believe). Lawns were

---

* The famous Indian diamond of 106 carats in weight; but in this context perhaps also the Persian *kohinur*, signifying "a mountain of light" requiring a steep ascent out of an abyss (see also p. 70 below).

planted in front of the blocks, surrounded by beds of pansies. Juniper bushes and Japanese quinces bordered the paths, and one corner actually featured pillows of forget-me-nots in the apparent desire that Auschwitz should remain indelibly stamped on our memories. The weather was glorious. The rays of the sun were cradled on the fresh green of the bushes, and from the south beckoned the mighty heights of the Beskids in the western Carpathian Mountains.

The polished facades and the heralds of spring must have caught me in their spell somehow, for I suddenly began to take hope again (perhaps because I still believed I would survive, in spite of every rational cell in my brain). In any case, it did mind and ears good not to talk about the chimneys for a change. Thus full of confidence, I happened to be talking to a French colleague of mine while we walked along one of the camp streets. I was making plans for the future: what we all would do once we were out in the world again, how we would enjoy our lives at some later date, and that we ought to set up a memorial for the victims of Auschwitz. He looked at me in disbelief, as if he hadn't understood a word I said. He kept his silence until we came to the end of the road. Then he said: "I'll tell you a little story, but in French, because it sounds better that way." He came from the Provence; he combined his native culture and amiability with a southern temperament and spoke very eloquent French.

"A man had died and was waiting to enter the Gates of Heaven. While he was standing there, the earth opened up before him and he saw deep down into the Kingdom of Hell. The souls of the departed were sitting around an extravagantly decked table, regaling themselves and enjoying a glorious meal. The table was dripping with delicacies, including the choicest of fruits, and was decorated with fantastic flowers; fine wine sparkled in the goblets. Beautiful women in elegant garments danced seductively around them; a pleasant melody wafted through the room and echoed off the walls. Boisterous merriment as far as the eye could see. The man at the Gates of Heaven watched in astonishment, heard how the guests below were calling to him and praising the Kingdom of Hell. So, when the Gates of Heaven opened, the man simply and unpretentiously requested that they let him go to the Realm of the Devil. The angel hesitated and painted the black abysses of the deep with terrifying words, but the newcomer continued to beg until he was granted entry to Hell. Once there, he was cast into a dark hole, tied to a glowing anvil, beaten with iron rods, and pinched with pointed tongs. He beseeched his tormentors to let him join the guests at the glorious feast in the part of Hell he had seen earlier. That's when they told him all that was only propaganda.

"That's the way it is here," he continued. "Everything is just propaganda meant to deceive us. They plant grass and flowers, paint the blocks—it's all for show; they'll still kill us. I could promise you a thousand pounds for an Auschwitz memorial. It's no lie; all my life I worked hard and saved what I could, and the money is right now lying in a bank in London. But I'll promise you even more. I'll promise you, in writing, the Kohinoor—you know, the largest diamond in the world—if we survive. And I'm just as sure that I'll never have to deliver on this promise."

He was right. I never will get the Kohinoor.

Curds and Whey

YOU'LL SOONER GET a loaf of bread from someone who has two and a half loaves or from someone who has only one than you'll ever get a slice from the person who has two large loaves to call his own. And it's easier to give away your third shirt as long as you keep one extra one for yourself than it is to break into a round dozen. So it was in the camp, as well. There were always the poor ones who did what they could to help others. From the wealthy you couldn't expect to get much more than what they threw away: the stem and the wilted leaves of their cabbage, the bowl of camp soup that they themselves disdained. Later, when the huge tubs of farmer's cheese were taxied in and the high gentlemen in the Gypsy camp had grown sick of it, they generously passed it on to us physicians who, between diarrhea and the edema of starvation, were balancing unsteadily on the edge of life. We ate these curds for months on end and were grateful to get them. In cool weather it was a refreshing treat with its delicious aroma of sour cream; on hot days the fermented mass stank most foully from its barrels and supported a crawling biological life of its own. Nevertheless, it was protein, and what's more, it could be shaped into clumps and served as our unvarying evening meal.

Cooking was forbidden in the concentration camp, but that didn't mean much. Living wasn't allowed either, and we tried that, too. Cooking, though, was difficult. It went well enough on those winter days when the large stove in the block was stoked on either end, when the water boiled quickly and a potato, if we were lucky enough to have one, was done in five minutes. At other times we had to make do with small, improvised "stoves": we painstakingly collected each individual piece of coal and every splinter of wood we could salvage from the boards of disintegrated bunks, sometimes even a piece of the storeroom wall. Then, since we didn't have any matches, someone brought a flame from somewhere on a twisted piece of paper. When we'd finally started a fire and everything was ready to go, we'd hear:

"The camp doctor!" He made a point of coming at different times—at some ungodly early hour in the morning or, often enough, again late in the afternoon and in the evening. (Our lookout system functioned well because we all had an equal stake in the outcome.) Immediately we extinguished the fire and stashed everything away beneath the straw mattresses on the bunks or in not very appetizing corners of the laboratory. Once he left we started all over again. Our choice of ingredients was rather limited: curds, bread in place of meal, sometimes a few boiled potatoes, salt, and a smidgen of margarine collected from what each of us could spare from earlier in the day. One Czech physician, a born jack-of-all-trades not unskilled in household matters, who also knew how to install stovepipes, run electrical wiring, and once in a while drum up something edible, was the cook. The others helped by fetching water, peeling and mashing the potatoes, breaking the bread into bits and rolling them with a bottle to make bread crumbs. Our cook kneaded the dough himself and carefully shaped it into clumps of painstakingly equal size. Then he tossed them into the boiling water and never let them out of sight until, one after the other, they bobbed to the top. He removed them cautiously and warmed them on the stove plate until the rest were ready. Finally, he sprinkled them all with bread crumbs browned in margarine. Our cook stood there for two, sometimes three hours, his face a bright red and the sweat streaming from his every pore. Then he served the dumplings to the whole company, each person's ration meticulously counted out. We ate them as reverently as he had prepared them, and declared them delicious. To vary things a bit, he sometimes made them round, sometimes oval, and sometimes flat; one shape tasted better than the other and we were full of praise for our cook.

We relished everything we got in the camp, even the monotonous unseasoned camp soup that consisted of turnips and barley and nothing else. And we took as much delight in material things as we did in edible ones. Each piece of clothing was an event, like the worn-out winter coat that a Polish Jew whom I didn't know had given me in January after the great cold spell, or the hand-knitted socks from Irene, who never stopped reading St. Francis of Assisi, even in Auschwitz. The knife, the foggy mirror—everything became a treasured possession. I wonder if Fiek will ever be as happy with her closetful of clothes as she was with her birthday present in the camp: that light blue nightgown with the colorfully embroidered collar.

Das Sonderkommando*

THERE WERE A NUMBER of labor detachments in Auschwitz, good ones and bad. Work in the kitchen and in the warehouses was most desired because, when threatened by starvation, it's a pleasant duty to hold in one's hands not only one's own bowl but that of the others as well and to be able to fill and empty it according to whim. Other coveted assignments were work in the clerical offices and in the "sauna," the bathhouse. These were respected positions that did not require a great deal of physical exertion; those in the offices were occasionally the site of behind-the-scenes influencing of prisoner transfers, while the ones in the sauna were very profitable. The sauna

---

* The *Sonderkommando* (Special Detail) was the inmate work crew that assisted in gassing and cremating "selected" inmates and new arrivals not admitted to the camps. See pp. 79 below and also Notes 37 and 38.

The prisoners in uniforms are members of the unit called "Canada," assigned to clear the boxcars of luggage and debris—a much sought-after position, since it presented the possibility of finding food and other valuables in abandoned parcels. The prisoners were searched after each shift, however, and severely punished if caught with any booty. Thus, as they worked they had to surreptitiously swallow whatever they found. Yad Vasham Photo Archives.

girls worked in the room where the new arrivals were forced to strip and abandon whatever they were wearing. Hence, the room came to resemble a fashion salon of sorts, where the girls had their choice of the best and the most beautiful. An even better opportunity for such "organization," which was the term we used to denote all sorts of undercover wheeling, dealing, and looting among the prisoners, was assignment to the "Canada" commando. These men and women worked in the sorting houses (we called them "Canada") that received the initial possessions the new arrivals were forced to abandon on the spot. Their task was to clear away and sort through all the baggage the new arrivals had brought with them and were ordered by the SS to leave at the railroad sidings. This included not only clothes but everything else a person well equipped for evacuation had dragged along: groceries, sometimes even the choicest delicacies, such as canned sardines, chocolate, cakes, and jam; cigarettes; soap; now and again a bottle of brandy; and, last but not least, books. Money was also a frequent find. The tailor in the Gypsy camp lived close to the platform by the railroad siding and enjoyed the patronage of both the SS and the prisoners. He once showed me 6,000 marks' worth of foreign currency in pengös, kronen, and francs. It represented one particularly good week's worth of loot.

Some people may be inclined to judge this behavior low and sordid—one group of prisoners pouncing upon what another group had to abandon with aching hearts, and not only material or sentimental treasures but things they so direly needed for their own survival. We must never forget that these were things that would all be confiscated by the SS, anyway, and lost to the prisoners in any case. What the Canada people managed to nab from all of this benefited not just them personally but, indirectly, the whole camp, through barter or presents. The acquisitions of the Canada detachment were a valuable addition to camp life, even if this was not immediately apparent on an individual basis. All of our few possessions, every comb and every toothbrush, came from this source. Effective medications could be gotten nowhere else. These seemingly simple salvaging efforts were fraught with danger, and the Canada people frequently paid for them dearly. Although they were allowed to stuff their mouths at will while at work, their pockets were out of bounds. On their daily march back to camp they were subjected to thorough and repeated "body searches": once at the camp gate, then at the bathhouse, and again in front of their block. If anything was found, the punishment was severe. Nevertheless, assignment to this labor detachment was highly desirable.

Another prime assignment was the band or orchestra, a labor detachment not unknown in concentration camps. The "music" had something of the quality of a pampered lapdog of the camp directorate, and the musicians were openly favored. Their block was even better tended than the clerical offices or the kitchen; food was abundant, and the girls of the women's band were issued neat blue woolen dresses and matching caps. The musicians were kept busy: they played at roll call, for instance, when the exhausted women returning from work had to march in time to the music, while the men, so overworked they could hardly drag themselves forward, were required to swing their legs in goose-step fashion. Music accompanied every official event: the harangues of the camp leader, the transports, and the formal executions whenever someone was hanged. In between, it served to entertain the SS and the prisoners in the infirmary. The band played every Tuesday and Friday afternoon in the area next to the women's camp, undeterred by the events and selections going on all around. And the musicians from the neighboring men's camp

Prisoners sort and transfer personal belongings left by prisoners after the arrival of a transport. Camp inmates referred to looted property as "Canada," associating it with the riches symbolized by Canada. Storage facilities for "Canada" occupied several dozen buildings around the camp. Yad Vasham Photo Archives.

used to play for the sick Gypsies as a final gesture before they died. The players were Dutch and French Jews, two of them renowned violinists. They performed popular songs and operetta tunes as a result of once having been deprived of their rations and ordered to stand for hours on end as punishment for playing Brahms and Bach during one of the obligatory Sunday morning serenades; the SS hadn't found the classical program entertaining enough. In spite of the cheerful melodies, the strings of their instruments quivered with heartbreak, and I'm not sure what was more difficult: to listen to the music in the camp, or to play it.

Those were the so-called good detachments, to which only very few prisoners, the particularly lucky ones, were assigned. I mention them only for curiosity's sake. The actual labor detachments were of a totally different nature and unremittingly ghastly. The one common feature was hard, physically annihilating, incessantly scurrying drudgery, to which the Kapos* mercilessly drove the prisoners with whips in hand. The work in the munitions factories and in the mills might have been almost bearable, but it included the hours spent in roll call and a rigorous punishment if the prescribed quota was not met. The external detachments made even greater demands on the emaciated bodies, which none of them could withstand for any length of time; these tasks included pushing wheelbarrows, working in the potato bunker, digging graves in deep mud, and making clearings along the banks of the Vistula River with a round-trip march of ten to fifteen kilometers a day. Every detachment was accompanied to and from work by a group of SS guards because the inner and outer sentry fences surrounding the camp could not be passed without SS supervision. Not infrequently, one of these guards would send a newly arrived prisoner, not yet familiar with the ways of the camp, half in jest and under some pretext or other, out beyond these encirclements. Once the prisoner managed to get beyond the fence, he would be "shot down in flight."

---

* The plural of *Kapo*. In camp language a male or female prisoner supervising a work detail. The word has no exactly corresponding word in pre-Nazi German, but may derive from the verb *kaprizieren,* meaning "to act capriciously and brutally."

And then there was that special detachment whose special tasks lent it the designation *Sonderkommando.* Young, strong, exclusively Jewish men were chosen for this detachment: fine, energetic young fellows. They learned the nature of their labor only after they had been transferred to another block. The Sonderkommando, like so many other detachments, had a block of its own, the only difference being that it was cut off from the rest of the camp. The isolation was so complete that no communication of any kind was possible. This detachment had the ghoulish task of working in the crematorium. As far as we were able to learn, they had to clear away whatever the unfortunates who were immediately sent to the gas had brought with them into the death chamber; this included their clothing as well as any last personal belongings. They had to stack the corpses of the gassed in alternating layers of wood to feed the big fires. Despite every effort at isolation, word got out that many of them rediscovered their families there, their parents, their siblings, often both together.

Sometimes they came to our camp to bathe, closely guarded by SS brandishing loaded revolvers and surrounded by huge, vicious dogs. Their faces were no longer human, but distorted, wild masks, so much so that one could have shrieked for horror. By the way, they were well paid for their labors. They were allowed to take whatever they wanted from the booty, including cigarettes and brandy. On the other hand, they had their own death sentence in their pocket. After one, two, or three months on the job they were themselves sent to the gas in order to assure and maintain an eternal silence. Sometime while at work, one never knew when, the valves of the gas chamber would close, the gas would be turned on, and—a new Sonderkommando would replace the old.[37]

One day toward the end of 1944 the Sonderkommando managed to blow up one of the crematoria, but only partially. Of the 302 men who fled, 300 were caught. They and the three girls in the munitions factory who had provided the explosives died a gruesome death.[38]

To subject human beings to perversions and atrocities such as this and to drive them to the ultimate perdition of their souls is the work of the devil. If the SS had created nothing more than the Sonderkommando in Auschwitz, this alone would have sealed their doom.

The Pilgrimage to Death

THE FIRST HUNGARIAN JEWS came to Auschwitz on May 17, 1944, and from then on until the beginning of July, six to seven freight trains arrived on a regular schedule, day after day, each transporting between twelve hundred and two thousand "passengers."[39] This word may be a bit inappropriate to describe people who had spent more than a week stuffed together in cattle cars so tightly as to be hardly able to breathe. What was still bearable in the early months soon turned into a death trap. The summer heat became so intense that one single car once contained forty dead bodies. When the doors finally opened, the survivors, parched and overcome by thirst, threw themselves like unclean animals on the slimy water of the puddles lining the railroad tracks. The food these new arrivals had brought with them, which the prisoners of the Canada detachment would ordinarily pounce upon, remained where it fell and was left untouched because it had been swimming in seas of excrement amongst the dead and the dying in the cattle cars.

We were able to witness every detail of these arrivals because the final destination was no longer Auschwitz, as it was when we arrived,

Jews arrive at Auschwitz-Birkenau from Hungary. Many of the Jews deported to Auschwitz from Hungary were not in fact Hungarian, but came from parts of Slovakia and Transylvania annexed by Hungary earlier in the war. This particular train delivered approximately three thousand Carpathian Jews, who had been en route for two and a half days with little food or water and only buckets for sanitation purposes. Yad Vasham Photo Archives.

but rather Birkenau, or more precisely: end station "Crematorium." This because the stop was hardly a hundred meters away from the first two crematoria. (In the end, the frequently discussed plan of leading the train right up to the crematoria and constructing an escalator feeding directly into the gas chambers was never realized.) We watched as the people stood in the middle of the main street of Birkenau, their abandoned packs and sacks scattered about,

The Hungarian women and children in this photograph stand in line awaiting "selection"—a decision whether they would live or die—at Auschwitz, probably in May 1944, at the height of the Hungarian deportations. Yad Vasham Photo Archives.

thoroughly drenched by the rain or, more frequently, withering in the sun, with their children restlessly bopping here and there or clambering down the grass embankment. We used to count the baby carriages.

It was a long train with people of all ages wearing every conceivable national costume from unsophisticated country clothes to custom-made city attire. There were men and even more women with children. Finally, after hours of waiting, the sharp command of the SS sent this particular train on its way, and we watched the people line up in rows one behind the other, the women now holding their children fast to their sides. The train disappeared momentarily behind the trees that lined the curve of the road behind Birkenau and then reappeared on the other side. Several troops of prisoners headed off toward the first crematorium, came to a halt, and waited there like hungry people in front of a grocery store or the way people stand in line for theater tickets, waiting for the doors to open. The remaining groups continued down the road that ran along the Gypsy camp to Brescinke: they marched between lush green meadows and fields of yellow rapeseed, their stumbling children at their side, and all those baby carriages raising only a slight puff of dust compared to the clouds thrown up by the SS automobiles speeding by. An endless procession of people.

We watched these marches day after day. The people were different, but the image remained the same: so many pilgrims on their way. We lost sight of them near the Brescinke Forest, and less than an hour later the flames rose high behind these woods. Two pillars of fire soared to the heavens. And the yard in front of the crematorium, where these people had been standing, where they had been waiting to enter their gas chambers, was deserted except for the flaming glow that never failed to appear punctually one hour after their entry. It shimmered through the otherwise so harmless-looking side windows, so unsuspicious in their blankness, and licked its way up the towering chimneys. Five huge flames burned day and night, and when they were extinguished, more victims arrived to fuel them anew—a reddish-yellow conflagration of wood and humanity. The sky was red from the glow and the stars paled behind it. The air was contaminated by the stench of burning bodies and singeing hair, and

These Hungarian Jewish women and children, unaware that they have been selected for death in the gas chamber, wait in the nearby wooded area next to the killing facility. Yad Vasham Photo Archives.

the smoke descended on the camp in swathes of ashes. Baal, the Assyrian fire god, was an amateur compared to Hitler, the god of the Nazis. And the funeral pyres of the Middle Ages were paltry, bungling efforts compared to the monster fires that were kindled in Auschwitz with the regularity of a factory engaged in continuous (and not always completely effective) gassings.

When we woke from our sleep at night—we who witnessed all of this and yet continued to eat and sleep like normal people—the inside walls of our block were lit up with the reflection of the blaze. And when I got up and crept out the back doors of the block that faced the crematorium opposite and looked toward the second one,

I saw the flames of the open fire next to it and watched as they tossed the dead (and sometimes not quite dead) bodies of the children onto it. I heard their screams, saw how the fire lapped at their tender bodies. No metamorphosis of my being, regardless of whether in this life or the next, will ever expunge this horror from my soul.

There were days when we couldn't see the flames any more, when we couldn't taste the heavy stench of burning any more. Even so, there was no escaping this purgatory of deepest hell that banished us behind electrified barbed wire. One day—it happened to be the 3rd of June and the sixteenth day of this continuous inferno—I ran amok. I railed against my God for the second time during my stay in the camp. I had long since come to terms with my own death, but why did such things have to happen at all and why did so many innocent people have to dissolve in smoke? Gradually, very gradually, I began to realize that no one dies in vain and no one perishes senselessly. I began to realize that we are all absorbed into the whole and that the life of a community, like that of an individual, strives toward an inner, not always obvious and visible, goal. We who are but ephemeral guests in the history of world events do not always witness the final act of reconciliation and can only surmise that these pilgrims on the road to death, five hundred thousand within a period of six weeks, were also journeying down one of God's paths.[40]

In the Sauna

A BRIEF TEN MINUTES, fleeting and soon lost in the long, never-ending saga of the concentration camp with its many weightier and more grisly experiences, and yet this small incident in the "sauna," in the bathhouse, remains in my memory and still leaves a choking sensation in my throat. It was sometime in July 1944; I can't be more precise than that except to say that the camp leader and members of the camp directorate had spent much longer than usual roaming about in the Gypsy camp and that it happened at 5:30 that afternoon.

The high point of the day for us prisoners occurred three times a week, between five and six o'clock, when we reported for our regularly scheduled "nurses' bath," replete with hot showers, thanks to a well-meaning Kapo. This man was a politically ostracized German who responded to a few kind words with even friendlier ones and, unlike other camps, where the water was distributed sparingly and accompanied by blows, he let the warm showers flow over our naked bodies in generous streams.

We undressed at five and waited for the doors to open. Twenty-two of us went under the shower, laughing and splashing about, dripping from head to toe and rejoicing in the delightful sensation of being able to indulge our bodies. And that's how Herr Schwarzhuber from the camp directorate found us while making his rounds. This SS officer inspected us not only in a patronizing, offhanded, and condescending way, but as a man in an appraising, smirking, and lascivious manner. He interrogated the naked women one after the other as to their origin, identification number, and their work in the camp, all the while gazing at the contours of our bodies, his eyes measuring our breasts and hips. And we were forced to respond to the quips and queries of this cooing man in his SS uniform with our unadorned words and naked bodies, for this, too, was part of what it meant to be a prisoner in Birkenau.

Gypsy Night

IN JULY 1944 the mood in the Gypsy camp was more tense than usual. The camp was no longer as large as it once had been. Of the twenty thousand Gypsies, most of whom were imprisoned in March of 1943 with a smaller contingent arriving later, only six thousand were left. Now the camp physician was singling out those of the group who were still able to work and assigning them to a transport. According to our sources, they were sent to the main camp in Auschwitz, where they were then divided up and dispatched to work camps or factories. The removal of workers from a camp was always an evil omen, especially when, as in this instance, the women and children were left behind. Equally ominous was the fact that the camp physician, who was particularly interested in the study of twins and anthropological measurements, ordered his medical experiments to be concluded as soon as possible.

Toward the end of July the air was heavy and humid. Gypsy halfcastes and the relatives of frontline soldiers were hastily evacuated from the camp. Some of the Polish nursing staff were relieved of their duties and transferred elsewhere. And the camp leader, who ordinarily appeared only sporadically, performed inspections of sinister frequency and duration. Something was in the air, and yet it couldn't have been anything too urgent, because the camp physician was concentrating more intensely than usual on his studies. He even went so far as to give us an ultimatum to cure the conjunctivitis that was plaguing so many of the children. And then, starting on July 28th, two large pots of children's soup were delivered as a daily supplement to the orphans' block.

July 31, 1944,[41] was a Monday, and it brought new surprises in the afternoon. The train carrying the Gypsies who had already been sent to the main camp returned to the Gypsy camp in Birkenau before it set out on its further travels from Auschwitz. This in itself was unusual enough, but the SS even gave the Gypsies permission, despite the block confinement, to gather on the platform and to talk to the prisoners on the train. It was a first in the history of the concentration camp. In the presence of the SS, people on both sides of the fence shouted out greetings over the thirty meters separating the two groups; they tossed packages and cigarettes and waved to each other as if taking leave at a train station in earlier and better times. The camp physician, who was standing by, calmly watched the scene and smiled at two Gypsy boys who happened to be part of the transport. They had previously served as his adjutants, had always been with him, were frequently even allowed to accompany him on short automobile trips, and were used to telling him, in childish confidence, everything that was going on in the camp, right down to the last detail. Only after the train pulled out were the prisoners driven back to their blocks.

At four o'clock the camp physician again sifted through the children's block for those deemed able to work, and these were loaded off to Auschwitz together with the twins. After that, one event chased the other with lightning speed. At five o'clock the Polish, not the Jewish, physicians and nurses were ordered to assemble and were transferred to the neighboring men's camp; then the female nurses were sent to the women's concentration camp. I was the only female Jewish doctor left behind. Hardly had the staff, with the exception of the Jews, left the camp than the SS imposed the strictest block confinement. Before I could scurry back to my children in the orphans' block, the camp road was blocked off by SS officers with orders to shoot; they stood as if planted in narrow rows on both sides of the street. I quickly fled to my colleagues in the quarantine block with the feeling that, if this was it, then I'd take my last walk with them.

This block, the last one in the camp next to the sauna, was barred and bolted shut. I took the night watch over the patients in lieu of the nurses who had left. Two colleagues who had worked in the now deserted clerical offices were counting the index cards with the names of the block inhabitants in order to determine the stand. Although outwardly calm, their trembling fingers nervously flicked through the red cardboard slips, one after the other, again and again. This was probably the tenth time already, for they could never come to an accurate count. We will never know if it was 129 or 130. Even the patients knew what was going on. Besides the sick, there were twenty-five healthy women in the block, quarantined there with their children suffering from chicken pox and scarlet fever. Their composure was nothing short of amazing. Several were weeping softly to themselves, others were praying.

In the distance we could hear the cars coming and going and disappearing again into the silence. Eventually the comings and goings and the sound of screeching brakes grew nearer. Toward 10:30 they stopped in front of our block. Was this it? Our door remained bolted shut. As it happened, it wasn't our turn, but that of the orphans' block opposite us. We hear the curt orders of the SS, the screams of the children. I recognize a few of the voices: the older ones resist audibly, cry out for help, shriek, Traitors! Bastards! Murderers! A few minutes of this, then the trucks drive off and the screams fade away in the night.

Another half hour or so and the trucks return to our block again, but they drive by, turn in by the sauna and—stop in front of us. It's our turn. Whom will they take first, the Gypsies or the Jewish doctors? The doors are torn open, SS storm in, accompanied by four prisoners. I know one of them, a Pole by the name of Tomaczik. One night, while drunk out of his mind, he haunted the nurses' quarters;

another time, as Kapo, he brutally whipped his boys with a stick. The commanding officer calls for the staff personnel—are we supposed to lead off?—looks us over one at a time and asks how many we are. The evacuation begins. People are ripped out of their beds, packed like bundles and transported away. SS men and the four prisoners work together, each one keeping a count of his own people. We stand by and watch it all, helplessly. A few minutes later the block is empty. Each individual bed is checked one more time, sticks are poked around under the mattresses, every corner of the block is scanned with lights. Then they bolt the doors again and the SS disappear with their victims.

We remain behind, unscathed. We didn't eat and we didn't sleep that night, even though the keeper of the stores had generously supplied us with meat before they left—meat! We hadn't had meat for over a year.

Next morning (it was August 1st) the Gypsy camp, which just days before had counted between thirty-five hundred and four thousand heads, was deserted and, in contrast to its usual buzzing babble, silent. One woman had actually managed to find a hiding place, but she turned up later on and was delivered to the camp leader. Two children, one aged three and the other five, had slept through the whole thing all bundled up in their blankets. They emerged from the orphans' block the next morning, hand in hand and crying for fear and abandonment. They were sent on afterwards.

When people ask, "Why is this night different from all other nights?"* there is only one answer: "It was one of many." I was sent

---

* The first question, translated directly from the Hebrew, of the Passover Service (Mah nishtannah—"Why is this night different. . . . "). The Passover Hagga-

back to the women's concentration camp the next day, one day later than the others only because my transfer papers lacked the signature of the camp physician, to whom all the other doctors were subordinate. The other Jewish doctors, the men, stayed on in the Gypsy camp, which was soon filled up with Russians and Hungarian Jews.

---

dah contains the story of the Exodus from Egypt. Dr. Adelsberger writes with heavy irony within her Jewish tradition.

◆ PART FOUR ◆

The Mother and the Grandmother

SOON AFTER the sad fate of my Gypsy wards I was assigned to supervise the sick children in the women's concentration camp. There weren't many: one set of Jewish twins (because the camp physician was using them for his research),[42] some half-castes; the rest were Russian and Polish children.

In addition to my little patients I had a whole group of "camp kids" who had long since left childhood behind. The youngest was eighteen years old. At first there were four Dutch girls. Two of them, Ilse and Ruth, were given over to my care by a Dutch woman doctor. They were soon joined by Fiek and Truus, both of whom came to the camp already sick unto death. Ilse, a pretty woman of thirty-two, had come to Auschwitz with her husband. The last time she saw him was on the platform at the train station. Work and hunger, heat and physical abuse had destroyed her, both body and soul. Nevertheless, she made a good recovery in August during the time when the gassings were in full force in the women's camp.* When the selections seemed imminent again in September, she, still as thin as a rake, was under the greatest threat. If the camp physician should find her, she'd be lost. For this woman, everything depended upon where they would begin the selections, whether in the camp among the working prisoners or in the hospital block or in both at the same time, as fate would have it. If what had happened in the overcrowded camps was any indication, the compound surrounding the hospital block seemed to

---

* The time is summer 1944, when the gassings of the Hungarian Jews reached their peak. Some 445,000 of a population of more than 762,000 were liquidated between May 15 and July 19.

be in the greatest jeopardy this time around. Ilse had to disappear as quickly as possible. With a great deal of wheeling and dealing and behind-the-scenes string-pulling, she was eventually transferred to the mill. The work was easier there than in the external labor detachments, but, as if in exchange, the food was worse. For three days she tried to work, but her legs were so weak she could hardly manage the hike to the factory. She stumbled repeatedly, was beaten and dragged back to camp. Five days later she was once again taken into our area at exactly the time our selections were ending and had shifted their fury elsewhere. She had made it this time. The same maneuver was repeated weeks later, and even though it succeeded, the toll it took was too much for her. She perished a short time later from a combination of exhaustion and pleurisy.

Truus, the eighteen-year-old who had wanted so badly to live, fell victim to the selection straightaway because there was no way to hide the tuberculosis she had contracted in the camp.

There remained only Fiek and Ruth, who actually were not even people any more, but only carcasses of skin and bones, hardly sixty pounds each—appropriate fuel for the fires, according to SS regulations.[43] Fiek was also suffering from pneumonia and Ruth needed a walking cast because her wasted leg muscles no longer supported what weight she had. Nevertheless, both possessed an unconquerable energy and a devout optimism. They just had to survive. They were wangled into a series of experiments on the scientific study of the composition of blood under starvation. Prisoners involved in experiments were protected from selection and received an additional ration of milk, not enough to make them fat, but enough to keep them alive. Fiek and Ruth managed to improve somewhat under these conditions and courageously pitched in later when our family increased.

Five new camp kids were adopted: two German Jewish girls, swollen to distortion by the edema of starvation; a Polish girl; an emaciated Hungarian girl with dark brown, parchmentlike skin covered with leprosy; and a hair-thin, delicate Greek girl. She and Fiek were the only ones to survive. The others, who were snatched from the gas chambers and tended and cared for for months on end, died after the liberation because their destroyed bodies were unable to revive.

The two German Jewish girls with their swollen bellies were always despondent; it was perhaps out of pure presentiment that they refused to believe in rescue, and so they died. Even Ruth, the believer, who had such enormous control over her body and who in her last days wrote a grateful letter to her parents and recited the prayer for the dead on her own behalf, died, as did Mermelstein, the little Polish girl. She suffered from leprosy, a vitamin deficiency; week after week we fed her like a baby because she had lost the habit of eating and would no longer do it on her own. After a while, though, she developed such a ravenous appetite that she gulped down one bowl of camp soup after the other. Proud and cheerful, she wandered about the block, happy in her ability to walk again. She collapsed after the liberation and died of the complications attending starvation.[44]

Besides these problem children, I had two other camp kids of a completely different nature: two girls from Slovakia, and not from our immediate compound. They were among the very first prisoners to come to Auschwitz and were endowed with strength and courage and will, and tempered with a kindly and helpful disposition. They never failed. One night a fire broke out in their block. They and a few comrades quietly fetched some water, dragged over the pails of sand, and managed to put the fire out. They even covered the wall surrounding the singed planks, thus not only protecting against the danger of a full-fledged blaze but also protecting their fellow prisoners from punishment by the SS.

These two girls adopted me as their "camp mother," cared for me like daughters, and valiantly provided me with clothes and food whenever they could. Evening after evening, always supposing there was no block confinement, we would sit together in the little room assigned to the block elder and act as if we would come out of Auschwitz alive. None of us really believed this, but we passed the time forging plans for the future and discussing the one big problem: how to prevent a second Auschwitz. Even if I never see them again, I am sure they will both work on such a project.

It is only because the relations in the camp were so confused that I can speak of these children at all, and what I am going to say about the mother and the grandmother can only be understood against this background. The "mother" was fourteen and a half years old. By some inexplicable miracle she had managed to escape the clutches of the camp physician and the maws of the gas chambers during the regular transports from Theresienstadt[45] and was sent to the women's concentration camp along with the ones who'd been declared ablebodied. When these women, including this girl's own mother and sister, were sent on to another labor camp, she was left behind, alone. Since no one knew what to do with her, she was concealed in our compound just as the camp physician was called to conduct a selection. We were under orders to seat all patients on top of the stove (which also served as a bench) in preparation for his visit; any exception to this rule was out of the question. It was at this inauspicious moment that this slim, pale child, icy cold and trembling all over, appeared. Since the number of newcomers had already been recorded in the clerk's office, there was no way we could hide her. With a warm hot water bottle pressed against her stomach, a swallow of warm coffee, and two stinging slaps (from me) on each cheek to make them glow a bright red, she walked past the camp physician without hesitation. But, since it never rains but it pours, another child of the same age turned up three days later; she, too, was spared the gas chamber by a mere whim of fate.

The two girls shared the same bed; they got accustomed to each other and became like twins. They spoiled me rotten with all sorts of kindnesses, from polishing shoes to sewing on buttons. On one such occasion I let slip, "You two care for me like a mother," whereupon one of them declared herself my mother and the other my grandmother from that moment on. And that's the way it remained. In December 1944, after the selections in Auschwitz had stopped,[46] the mother and the grandmother were transferred to the children's block. The grandmother celebrated her fifteenth birthday there. They had saved up a full week's worth of whatever bread, margarine, or other rations they could spare so that they might invite me and offer me a cheese and sausage sandwich. It was without exception the most precious gift I have ever received in my life.

Some people might react to this incident with a condescending smile at such "childishness" and wonder if such were our cares in the concentration camp. Maybe they were. There were many families like this and everyone had her own. They were not motivated by trivialities, but rather by a genuine sense of solidarity among people who shared each other's grisly fate and felt responsible for one another. The very fact that people came together, stood up for one another, often putting their own lives in jeopardy by denying themselves the very morsel of bread they needed for their own survival, and that they formed a family more tightly knit than many a natural one, was something exceptional; and not only for those who survived, but also for the many for whom such friendship and the love of their comrades eased the horrors of their miserable end.

Motherhood

ACCORDING TO SS guidelines, every Jewish child automatically condemned his mother to death.[47]

Apart from individual chance occurrences, the camp did not keep Jewish children on. They were consigned to the fire, either living or gassed, immediately upon arrival, and they were not alone, for their mothers went with them. Every woman who had a child in tow, even if it wasn't her own but someone else's child whom she just happened to have under her care at the moment, was marked for death. Old, experienced prisoners frequently tried to shift children from their mothers to their grandmothers as soon as they got off the train; after all, the grandmother was already doomed because of her age. It was heartrending to see how the mothers who refused to be separated from their children pulled them back, sometimes unknowing but sometimes also knowing that it meant their common death; or to have to respond to the fathers in the first few days after their arrival when they awkwardly asked after their wives and children. How were we to tell these newcomers that their children's playground was no longer on this earth?

Pregnant women were frequently admitted to the camp; they included women from mixed marriages,[48] who were generally spared the gas chamber, and childless full Jews whose pregnancy was not detected when they arrived. A number of them were subjected to induced miscarriages as late as the fourth and fifth month without regard for the fact that an operation at this point was a medical mistake and that the artificially induced termination of pregnancy in healthy women is taboo all over the world.

The few pregnant Jewish women who escaped the gas as well as the coerced abortion gave birth in the camp. Just like the other women prisoners—the Russians, the Poles, the Slovaks—these Jewish women were transferred to the pregnancy block during the last weeks, without any increase in their rations, of course, and brought to the birthing station at the first signs of labor. There they received "medical and nursing" care, at least as far as was possible in a concentration camp, and the delivery proceeded normally. However, as soon as the newborn saw the light of day, the inconceivable happened: The Jewish child was forfeited to death, and with him, his mother. Within a week both were sent to the gas chamber.

Medical ethics prescribe that if, during labor, the mother and the child are in danger, priority must be given to saving the life of the mother. We prisoner physicians quietly acted in accordance with this regulation. The child had to die so that the life of the mother might be saved. (Many women never got over the shock of the death of their newborn infants and have forgiven neither themselves nor us.) We saved up all the poison we could find in the camp for this very purpose and it still wasn't enough. It's amazing what newborns can bear. They simply slept off otherwise lethal doses of poison, sometimes without any apparent damage. We never had enough for them.

One time there was no poison available, and so the mother strangled the child she had just delivered. It didn't die. She was a Pole, a good mother who loved her children more than anything else. But she had hidden three small children back home and wanted to live for them.

Between the Spheres

I HAD WORKED LATE one evening and was sitting in front of the block. The heavens were clear, glorious, and deep, as often happens in September, studded with countless sparkling points throughout the firmament and crisscrossed with meteors and shooting stars. The horizon dipped off in the unfathomable expanse. In front of me the smoking chimney, the yellow-red torch of human flesh. Behind me in the distance, like shadows, were sketched the contours of houses and the spire of a church. Silence and peace reigned supreme, punctuated only by the swelling and skipping tongues of flame and the meteors that danced in the sky and then disappeared from view. I trembled. What was real? The barbed-wire hell here, where human beings seethe in the fire, right next door to the sleeping blocks, or the heavens above with their dancing stars, or perhaps that other world outside and beyond the fence, where free men live and the day follows its usual routine? Is there even such a thing as that other world, where people snuggle up in their cozy beds, sit happily around the dinner table with people they love, where some might lie in the fields and others listen to the songs of birds or the music of Mozart? Or was all that just a fairy tale, the blessings of a nighttime dream that will never come again? Where is true existence? Not out there, for that world doesn't exist for us any more and our people are gone. Not in the camp, in the broilers of hell, because these fires, too, will die out. Nothing remains. Only the stars follow their unchanging paths and trace out a thread of eternity. And we exist, hovering over the abyss and still preserving in our hearts a great, unshakable belief in the Eternal Being.

Mala, the Belgian Woman

MALA, A BEAUTIFUL twenty-year-old Belgian Jew, ran away with a Polish man and actually managed to escape. A few weeks later they were recognized crossing the Slovakian border, arrested, and brought back to Auschwitz. The Pole was publicly hanged in the men's camp one October day. Mala was brought to trial in the women's camp. We all knew her. She had been in Auschwitz since the beginning of 1943 and had worked in the "political division," the highest position a prisoner could attain. We all liked her; even the SS people enjoyed her company. She was led into the camp under SS guard, her arms tied behind her back. She had just spent eight days in the penal bunker and looked tired and unstrung. Nevertheless, she put on a cheerful demeanor. SS men accompanied her to the roll call arena, where thousands of prisoners were ordered to witness the execution. The camp commandant spoke a few well-chosen words distinguishing between the good care obedient prisoners received and the punishment meted out to rebellious ones. Meanwhile, Mala had managed to loosen her hands and, like a flash, she pulled a small razor blade out of a tiny, almost invisible pocket. Before the surrounding SS men could stop her, she slit both wrists wide open. She slapped the commandant in the face with her bleeding right hand and shouted so that all could hear: "I'm going to die and I want to. But my people will live and all of you will perish!"

Her wounds were not bandaged. They carried her off to the crematorium with the blood streaming from open arteries. On the way she collapsed into unconsciousness.

Others went silently and quietly, but they, too, live on in our memories. Each one left behind a gesture, a salute, and a promise.

A Broken Leg

LEADING OFF the women in Auschwitz were a thousand German political prisoners and a transport of Jewish women from Czechoslova-
kia,* the latter all strong individuals who hailed from the country
and displayed the robust stature and native strength of people accustomed to wringing fruit from the earth with the sweat of their brows.
With nerves of steel, muscles of iron, and an inexhaustible vitality
they endured the trials of the concentration camp, from bullets to
whips to fits of feverish shivers and the drudgery of slavery, from
increasing hunger and thirst to the sight of the blood and the wasting
away of their loved ones. Several managed to stay alive and maintain
their strength until May of 1943, when I met them for the first time,
and even on into the fall of 1944, after having spent more than two
years in Auschwitz. Illonka was one of these women. She bore the
number 1100 on her left wrist, but no triangle, for she came before
they introduced this sign of the Jew and of annihilation.[49]

Illonka's first assignment was to a labor detachment working in
the swamp outside the camp; there she waded knee-deep in its filthy
waters with suppurating boils covering both her legs. She bore the
pain like a fakir and had only rags to tie around her festering wounds.
She had no bandages, for they would have betrayed her to the women
guards and the camp physician and would have sent her right up the
chimney. She was eventually transferred to "desk duty" in her second
year and worked as an aide to the block elder. Like the few other

---

* The phrase "Leading off" here denotes senior prisoners with low numbers
stamped on their left arms. They were accorded respect for their long survival,
some having arrived in Auschwitz as early as April 1942.

original prisoners, this block elder lived in a compound apart from the general camp, had sufficient food, and was envied by many. Newcomers who only noticed the larger piece of bread easily overlooked what these few had already endured and fulminated against the established prisoners in their privileged position. Several had been truly hardened under the weight of the blows they'd received; the licking tongues of the flames had singed their souls until nothing remained except the beast that wanted to live and eat, and hate against God and man, even against their fellow prisoners. On the other hand, many of them cultivated a compassion for others out of the depths of their own misfortune. Illonka was one of the ones who helped wherever and whenever she could.

She soon moved on from desk duty to another assignment, for nothing was permanent in a concentration camp where the prisoners were kept on edge by constant upheaval. She was ordered to serve as Kapo in overseeing the cesspool. This work brought with it a double ration of food and was physically light: all she had to do was stand there and watch as exhausted, starving women from every block lugged over the heavy, stinking pails, how they dug out the cesspool and loaded the waste onto dung trucks, which these human skeletons then dragged laboriously across the bumpy ground. Not to mention that the area surrounding the cesspool was saturated with the overflowing and oozing excrement and gave off a nauseating stench; the air was contaminated far and wide by the fumes of the feces. Illonka stood in the middle of it all and did her duty, her preferential duty.

It had rained a lot by the end of August and a slimy pool of urine encircled the sinkhole. Illonka lost her footing in the slop and fell right in front of the wooden wagon, which rolled over her ankle and shattered the bone. This, too, she bore without complaint; she was used to pain and the cast fit her well. But this time she was assigned to our area. Her fellow Czechs took care of her, provided everything she needed for her broken leg, and prepared a special dish for her every day. The leg healed well and on October 10th she was already able to limp around the infirmary with the help of a walking cast. The next day the camp physician examined her. He determined that she was no longer able-bodied and wrote her number in his book. She knew. On October 14, 1944, she was sent to the gas, after having spent more than two years in Auschwitz, and as part of the very last selection.

She didn't die alone. Among the many hundreds were five women from the Hindenburg Labor Camp. They had arrived the week before on suspicion of typhus—five big, strong women. No one ever found out who had hung this fatal suspicion on them. They lay in my ward, fever-free and healthy as could be from the first day on. When their numbers appeared on the list, I implored the camp physician to spare these healthy, strong women. He wouldn't do it.

Two Hungarians

I DIDN'T INVENT these next two women; they really lived in block 22 of the women's concentration camp in November 1944.

Gabbi had been transferred from the surgery to the "intensive care" unit following the lancing of a boil. Such a trivial event would have gone completely unnoticed in the camp a few months earlier, but she was not recovering and had succumbed to a complete passivity. She was not showing any serious pathological symptoms but remained unresponsive to care and treatment, crept listlessly beneath her blanket, and refused to eat. Very pretty with a good figure, a Ph.D. and a law degree by the time she was twenty-seven, this young woman was accustomed to social and professional success in Budapest and was coddled by family and friends alike. She simply refused to play Cinderella in Auschwitz. She died a few days later, not as the result of starvation or infection, not as the result of being beaten or bullied, but as the result of her own lack of will and her inability to adapt.[50]

The "bed" beneath her was assigned to Miriam. A passing stomach colic had brought her to the infirmary and would have sent her out again just as quickly if she hadn't established herself as—*sit venia verbo**—the Shitkapo. What this job entailed cannot be described in the words of a civilized language. Diarrhea, the camp disease, left its traces all over, in the bunks, in the passages, and especially where the patients stood in line before the pails and simply couldn't wait any longer; the floor was an undulating open sewer. This is where Miriam volunteered to work. She put her energy to the task, slaved from four in the morning until nine at night, fetched water from the distant washroom, thawed it out with a burning stick when it froze beneath her hands, and indefatigably cleaned the Augean stables. She was always calm and even-tempered and extremely polite to everyone in the six languages she had at her command. What no force and no threat could achieve, she accomplished through her friendly attitude and flexibility. The bog was gradually transformed into some kind of order. She got a second bowl of camp soup and a double ration of bread as official recognition of her labors; it kept her from starving and saved her life.

---

* The Latin tag marks a departure from the linguistic civility that is the hallmark of the memoir. It is a plea to the reader, best translated as "please pardon the expression."

Behind the Fence

ELECTRIFIED BARBED-WIRE FENCES not only encircled and separated Birkenau from the outside world but also isolated from each other the individual compounds that constituted the main camp. All of Birkenau was one elaborate, tightly knit wire web into which were stuffed prisoners who gradually became accustomed to many things in the camp, but never to these live-wire fences.

Being incarcerated in a dungeon and surrounded by solid, impenetrable walls may seem worse than being cut off by wires, but such cells can be penetrated now and again, either by an occasional visit or the chance letter. In Birkenau, too, the "imperial Germans," those from the Reich, and non-Jewish prisoners were allowed to write (and to receive packages) once or twice a month. Even if these heavily censored letters contained only stereotyped phrases about one and the same theme, namely, how well the prisoner was treated in Auschwitz, they nevertheless did represent a sign of life for loved ones on the outside. For the Jews there was no connection to the outside world. Whether one was healthy or sick, still steady on one's legs, close to death, or maybe even dead already, no news slipped through the wires. To the outside world we were dead and gone. The few postcards individual Jews did write, on order of the "politicals" and with the prescribed text, did nothing to change this reality. I was ordered to send such a postcard to Berlin on July 13, 1943. Still in the throes of typhus, dazed and stupefied, I could hardly guide the pen. Such was the state I was in when I scribbled the dictated message that told of my good health and praised the attractions of Birkenau near Neurin, which was how the official return address read. The fact that Birkenau was part of Auschwitz and a concentration camp was never mentioned. Later on, once Birkenau had become sufficiently infamous, the Hungarian Jews there had to date their cards from Walsee in Bavaria. We never learned what became of these postcards and never lost the suspicion that they were used as a *testimonium vitae** and a deceptive maneuver for subsequent transports.

It is only when one is hermetically sealed off from the rest of the world that one realizes how much our whole life and its content are tuned to this world. Our whole being has its purpose and sense only in relation to it. I often think of the story of the bishop in his cage during the French Revolution with a tinge of envy. Condemned to death, he was put in a spacious cage and suspended from the ceiling high above the courtroom. Whatever he needed by way of food and drink was pulleyed up to him, so generously that he became amorphously fat as a result of his enforced inactivity. He used the time in his prison cage to write a historical-philosophical work, which he left to his friends as his intellectual estate. Not even so much as a greeting from us could penetrate through the wire web to the outside world, no word of farewell and no testimony to that which took shape within us in the face of death.

As completely and absolutely cut off from the world as we were, the world itself was ever present and visible to us through this ubiquitous wire. With every breath we drew we could spy freedom through the electrified wires that formed an extended web more than three meters high and crosshatched with vertical wires at intervals of twenty centimeters throughout. The green fields and forests beck-

---

* The Latin words carry the full weight of a sworn testimony about the conditions of life in the camp.

This aerial photograph of Auschwitz-Birkenau was taken in September 1944, and enlarged and labeled by the CIA in 1978. The women's camp is on the left. Gas chambers are visible in the upper right. National Archives, Washington, D.C., courtesy of the U.S. Holocaust Memorial Museum.

oned on the other side, a mere one hundred paces away, and yet as inaccessible as the heavens. The mountains rose in the south; a journey of one or two days would have sufficed to bring us to the peaks where the birds fluttered freely—but no bird, no butterfly, no ant, no earthworm was ever seen in Birkenau. Even airplanes flew toward these mountains, but for the prisoners in Birkenau there was no path that led to them. We lived on another planet.[51] All our yearning recoiled on the inexorable wire. It dissected every image with harsh, horizontal lines. Every tree we could see bore iron notches in its trunk, and even the sun that sank low on the horizon was shredded by the barbs on the wire.

Even the prisoners in the neighboring camp were crosshatched by the wires separating us. They were so close and yet on an isolated island, just like us. The wire sawed through the closest of family bonds. Siblings, husbands, and wives lived in adjoining barracks and were not allowed to talk to each other; young people, greedy for life, who had already signed their pact with death, were boxed in next to each other and forbidden to love one another. Everything was separated by the live high-tension fences. Electric abrasions, small wounds and slight shocks, ripped-open skin and extensive burns were the order of the day. Moreover, these wire fences were studded with watchtowers, and from the heights the sharp eyes of the SS controlled every move we made. On the ground, sentries were posted at intervals of every few feet; their duty was to see to it that the fence was not disturbed. As soon as someone made a suspicious move or came too near the wire, he was shot, even the children whose tumbles and chases brought them too close. One day two dumb Gypsy boys were playing by the wire fence. One of them, a boy of five, was shot in the stomach and died of his wound; the other, an eight-year-old, had to have his right hand amputated.

Despite the danger, the prisoners couldn't stay away from the fences. Husbands and wives exchanged things between the wires, as did brothers and sisters, friends and lovers. In an unwatched fraction of a second the gleanings of the Canada commando flew over the fence—goodies they had confiscated from the trains and which they couldn't bring into the camp: a woolen blanket, a pair of shoes, a piece of bacon. This was where white bread and medications from the infirmary were passed on to the labor detachments in return for whatever they had managed to bring back from their workplace: a scrap of material, an unripe apple. Love letters were smuggled back and forth between the wires, stammering fragments of bottled-up passion, which spelled death for the one caught sending them. At the risk of their lives family members would send each other what little bread they themselves could hardly afford to spare.

We watched the Christmas party in the men's infirmary from our position as audience behind the fence. It was December 1944; the Russians were nearby and the members of the detachment were extraordinarily cheerful.[52] Physicians and nurses were allowed to strike up dance tunes with a jazz group. It was an open-air performance on the grassy area close to the wire. The women crowded around on the other side of the fence, shouting "Bravo!" and clapping their hands. The program was good, nothing was forbidden, no sentry shot into the crowd. Caged in as we were like wild animals, perhaps then more than ever before we knew what it meant to be "behind the fence."

The wire had only one redeeming aspect: when we couldn't go on any longer, it would deliver us. The euphemistic expression "I'm going to the wire" was no mere figure of speech in Birkenau.

• PART FIVE •

WORD OF THE ADVANCE of the Russian front toward the upper Silesian industrial centers reached even the prisoners in Birkenau. We learned that the Russians had stormed Katowice and Tarnów, cities hardly one hundred kilometers away from Auschwitz. We watched the many Russian fighter squadrons as they flew over our heads toward Germany, and it was with a feeling of euphoria that we followed the individual phases of an air battle near Tarnów in the early days of January 1945, a battle from which the Russians emerged victorious. We saw how the bombs pounded Auschwitz[53] and watched the towers of flame and the clouds of smoke rise high in the sky. Later that evening we learned that the bombs had spared all the prisoners' barracks in the area and had hit the SS field hospitals with hairsplitting precision, leveling them to the ground. That was the time one of those small miracles actually did happen: all the SS officers in the building were killed, but with the exception of a very few, all the prisoners who were working there were saved because they weren't allowed in the air raid shelters and had been driven out onto the open fields. From early January on, we were treated to (and actually enjoyed) the nightly lights-out order in the camp, for it confirmed our suspicion that we were indeed in Danger Zone I. The only thing we didn't know was how the whole adventure would end for us in the concentration camp. There were many rumors afloat that the Germans intended to bomb the camp flat at the very last moment in an effort to eliminate all traces and annihilate all witnesses. This rumor had a lot going for it. No wonder we were all suffering under the strains of enormous pressure.

On January 17th the whole world seemed to fly off its hinges. The camp directorate invited the Birkenau prisoners to a cabaret performance in Brescinke. We couldn't believe our ears. During the previous few weeks we'd heard about films being shown to the prisoners in the men's camp in Auschwitz, but a cabaret performance in Brescinke was something else again. What just two months earlier was the scene of the grisliest show on earth, replete with a fireworks display of human bodies, was now a stage featuring music, dance, and fashion shows. Whoever wanted to go was allowed to do so, and we were transported in a closed train under SS supervision. (Strangely enough, it never occurred to us that we might be on our way to the gas.)

The next surprise wasn't long in coming. We in the infirmary were awakened at one in the morning by a breathless messenger, who urgently demanded the card files together with the clinical records of all our patients. This was nothing extraordinary in itself, for with every transport of patients to another camp (up until now they had never included Jews), the clinical records had to be sent on as well, and the camp physicians set at us with a vengeance to see to it that we delivered them to the next compound complete and in impeccable order. This time, though, unlike before, the records weren't inspected but immediately crumpled up and thrown into a pile, which then was stuffed hastily into a sack, obviously with the intention of destroying all evidence of both prisoners and patients in Birkenau as quickly as possible. (Eight weeks earlier the books in the clerical offices had been confiscated, ostensibly because of a paper shortage; we were told they were to be pulped as waste paper.) This minor incident confirmed our suspicion that Birkenau was to disappear from the face of the earth; and it cost many people their lives.

January 18, 1945, is indelibly stamped on my memory, and will remain so even if I should live to be a thousand.[54] It was a Thursday. I'll never forget how we swung back and forth between the prospect of being murdered now, so close to the end after having survived all those years in the concentration camp, and the hope of being loaded on a transport that would take us, alive, out of Auschwitz. We improvised backpacks and shoulder bags out of old rags, collected and sorted all our possessions, and packed and repacked senselessly. Although already playing blind hooky with our own lives, we still tried to calm our bedridden and panic-stricken patients. One man, of whom I was very fond, lay critically ill in his barracks. There was no way he'd be able to go with us when we were marched off. Should I go or stay behind when the others left? To abandon him to his fate when I knew him to be in sure and mortal danger seemed nothing short of betrayal. On the other hand, did a person who had survived nearly two years of Auschwitz have the right to risk her life out of affection, especially when she had no hope of helping anyway? Wasn't it my duty to renounce all personal ties and go? All of these things were racing through my mind that night.

The official order in the morning read: "Transport." All sick prisoners were to be included as long as they were able to walk to Auschwitz, a distance of about three kilometers. That's what they said at first. Later they were talking about a fifteen-kilometer march. None of the selections in all those years was more distressing than this one, for the choice as to which of the patients would go on the march was up to us this time. Now that the door was open, we were the ones who were supposed to abandon the people we loved, leave behind the patients we had tended for months and had kept alive against all odds. We were still reeling under the pressure of this nocturnal intermezzo when a few Polish women happened to overhear an exchange between the camp physician and his staff through the thin walls of the laboratory. He wanted to know what provisions had been made for thousands of dead people. For us, the fate of the last prisoners of Birkenau was sealed.

The patients were examined again and again as to whether they could walk; they were sent back to bed only to be hauled out again and subjected to another attempt. Whoever wanted to go and didn't fall down was given the scantiest bit of clothing and shoes, often only wooden clogs. Many actually returned to their block after taking their first few steps along the camp avenue, disappointed, desperate. We wanted to carry one of our colleagues, who was still suffering from the effects of stomach typhus, on a stretcher. The camp physician forbade it, and she had to be returned to the barracks. The final farewell a short time later was a torture, for her eyes watched us go as she remained behind in the full expectation of certain death.

They summoned us to roll call and gave the marching orders over and over again, and each time nothing came of it. We never sat down and had nothing to eat that whole day. Finally, toward five o'clock in the evening our group set out under already twinkling stars. It was no dream. We who never believed it possible that we'd ever escape from the Auschwitz concentration camp were actually leaving Birkenau alive.

Many months later we learned that Auschwitz and Birkenau had been evacuated by the retreating Germans and were left almost untouched. The prisoners we'd been forced to leave behind almost at the cost of our sanity were liberated by the Russians on January 27, 1945—much sooner than all the others.[55]

A Hike through the Snow

A WISE WOMAN once said: "All wishes are fulfilled, but not always at the right time." I'd always longed to stroll through a snowy landscape under a full moon, but I would have preferred to have done so under different circumstances; when my chance came, it wasn't the way I'd imagined it.

The gates of Birkenau closed behind us, and we were marched toward Auschwitz. It took us close to an hour to cover the three kilometers because we were heavily laden with the blankets we were bundled up in, the bread we'd managed to find and take from the warehouses, and our paltry possessions. They weighed heavier on our shoulders than ever in their hour of use. Those who had been sent to Birkenau immediately after getting off the train or had been expedited directly to Birkenau, and there were many of us who fit this description, saw Auschwitz for the first time that night. Even today, the very mention of that name makes my blood run cold, but my mind's eye sees it, strangely enough, as a fascinating stage set. Perhaps the sense that we were leaving the concentration camp alive in spite of the overwhelming odds and were actually leaving forever, perhaps the newly planted and hardly appropriate hope of liberation transfigured the final impression, or maybe Auschwitz really was bewitchingly beautiful that night. The moon bathed everything in its glow. The tall stone houses that seemed so enormous to us compared to the low barracks soared high into the sky, the sharp corners of their roofs sliced the horizon and stood out like hulks against the broad snow-covered fields that sparkled magically in the moonlight. In the shadows below, the narrow path snaked its way between bluish walls, bordered on both sides

"Arbeit Macht Frei," or "Work Makes You Free," was the slogan that greeted new arrivals to Auschwitz-Birkenau. This photo of the main gate was taken sometime after January 1945. Main Commission for the Investigation of Nazi War Crimes, Warsaw, courtesy of the U.S. Holocaust Memorial Museum.

by the wire fence that surrounded the buildings and no longer enclosed us on the other side. The ghostly sentries marching up and down along the fence were no longer keeping guard over us; they seemed like unreal figures whimsically scattered here and there in a child's drawing. Between them the column of thousands of people poured slowly around the bends, this time not toward the gas chambers but away from them, an endless train of people who came and went like so many eternal extras on a stage. It took more than two hours for this mass of people, close to ten thousand in all, to make their way along the narrow paths, held up as they were by the SS, who were distributing rations along the way: one can of meat for every two people. Perhaps the most unnerving thing of all was the friendly manner in which they did so.

Thus equipped, we set out on our march along the highway. Only now, after not having been loaded onto the wooden biers in Auschwitz and not having been shot, only now did our secret fears begin to fade away and were we finally able to breathe a little more easily.

It really was a moonlit midnight stroll in the snow. The deep, starry sky radiated high above us, the moon beamed in full glory, the snow nestled down like a huge velvet carpet over the fields and meadows, the forests shimmered phantasmagoric whiteness, and the ice crystals glittered on the branches like filagree. The snow lay deep on the road and crunched under our every step. We marched the whole night through and at first enjoyed our journey in the open air with the joy only someone who'd been imprisoned for years can appreciate. One or another of us, especially those who overestimated their strength and became weary, sat down in the snow to rest a while before catching up later; some even decided to return to Auschwitz at a more moderate pace. The only disturbance in our sense of freedom was the many sentries marching at our side, one to the right and one to the left at intervals of every ten rows.

At dawn the sun rose from behind the Beskids as we continued to plod along through the snow, now no longer so cheerful, for we were already tired and hungry and desperate for a rest. But the road led ever uphill and down and, by the position of the sun, sometimes to the south, the west, the north, always through the soft, deep snow, without rest, without pause, without end: nothing but snowscape, punctuated here and there by a dead body or two. They lay on the side of the road, along the inclines of the shoulders and on top of snow drifts, all with bleeding head wounds: women and men, some in civilian clothes, some in blue-and-grey-striped prisoners' uniforms, all with their sacks and packs, and each with a number. At first we couldn't imagine how they might have met such an end out here, but there were soon more and more of them, until finally they lined the road in intervals of every few feet. The longer we marched and the heavier it became to drag our weary limbs, the more we came to realize that these were the prisoners of Auschwitz, the ones who had set out before us and whose strength had finally given out; now they were left lying in the snow. Our own ranks soon began to thin out as well, and now and again we heard the snap of the dreaded pistol. Whoever couldn't continue was shot on the spot. Once it was the twin of a girl who tried in vain to urge her exhausted sister onward; another time it was a mother before the very eyes of her daughter.[56]

So this was the end. For this we had suffered through the long years at Auschwitz. But we continued to stomp on through the snow, and the sides of the road were sprinkled red with blood.

Before us and behind us the road went round in circles. We had already marched more than fifty kilometers by the time we passed the village of Pless* at noon on January 19th; here, long rows of wagons, each piled high with disorderly heaps of hastily gathered belong-

---

* German for the small Polish town Pszczyna, about thirty kilometers south of Katowice and due north of Auschwitz.

ings, lined the road; cattle grazed and hay accumulated, and the village showed all the signs of having been abandoned in a hurry. We dragged on past Prince's Park in Pless, famous for its monuments, casting hardly a glance through the barred gates, until we reached an open field behind the town where we stopped for a brief rest. Before we could gulp down a chunk of bread and slurp up a handful of snow to soothe our parched throats, the relentless SS ordered us on our feet and forced us onward, mercilessly executing the stragglers. After twenty-six hours of uninterrupted tramping we stopped the next evening in a small hamlet, where the thousands of people were crammed into a few barns. We had nothing on hand to eat because most of us had cast off everything we were carrying along the way out of pure exhaustion. (The next time I'm evacuated from a concentration camp, the only things I'll take along will be cigarettes, sugar, a toothbrush, and a comb, always supposing I have them.)

We set out early the next morning. Tired, exhausted, famished, and chilled to the bone—it was a little above freezing—we marched on: forward, then back again, without any discernible direction. For one long, never-ending day we simply ran for our lives. Toward seven that evening we reached Loslau,* covering the last ten kilometers running double-time and consuming our last ounce of strength. Our column of emaciated prisoners of Auschwitz, many of them sick, and with seventy children in tow, had covered about one hundred kilometers over hills and through valleys, all the while wading through deep snow and always only one step ahead of death.

---

* Mention of Loslau indicates a turning due east to reach the railhead where the tens of thousands of evacuees were divided into groups for shipment to various camps in Germany and Austria.

And we still hadn't reached our destination. On the morning of January 21st, after a night of struggles among the much-too-many of us, all trying to find a spot in the straw to sit and warm ourselves, we were led to the train station and packed into open coal cars. We were shoved in in masses, and more on top of them. The doors were barred shut. Between 120 and 130 individuals were stuffed into each coal car; we couldn't even stand because of the crush, let alone sit. The weather was frigid. The sharp cold tore at our skin, whittled away at our fingers and toes, and drilled into our lungs and entrails with every breath we took. Ravenous hunger gnawed away at our hearts. We stretched out our days with the last crumbs we could peel out of our pockets and quenched our thirst with the snow we scratched and scraped off the dirty sides of the coal cars. Whenever the train halted in an open stretch, a few agile girls climbed quickly over the edge of the car, filled their bowls with snow, and carried them back. A fierce struggle broke out for every handful, and not only for the snow but for the tiniest bit of space thus liberated in the car. It may be that our being so crowded together is what saved us from freezing to death, but after the exertions of the march, this constant defending yourself against being crushed to death used up whatever reserves we might have had left. One of the SS men assigned to guard us was carried out unconscious after two days, and six people were trampled to death in one single car.

The journey continued for six days and six nights, with no end in sight. We didn't know where we were going or how long it would take to get there. We noted each station with growing anxiety: we passed Breslau and Frankfurt an der Oder, where hordes of people had set up camp around the train station, and the trains, full to bursting, rumbled on toward the west. We continued on toward Sagan and through the eastern suburbs of Berlin. Then we rolled past Oranienburg and Fürstenberg on toward Ravensbrück. There, in one of the most infamous of all the concentration camps, where hecatombs of prisoners had been brutally slaughtered since 1933, there we were finally unloaded after a journey whose start was marked by so much hope.[57]

We lay for a full day in the dirty snow piled high against the walls of the camp avenue, still without food or drink. (Some people were offering a golden chain, even a watch, for one glass of water.) Toward evening eight thousand people were herded into a machine shed, where a bowl of camp soup and a few potatoes awaited those skilled in pushing and shoving their way to the front.

* * *

I DON'T THINK more than 15 or 20 percent of the women on the march gave out, but that's an awful statistic in itself. Even so, it's still relatively small when one considers the condition these people were in when they left Auschwitz. In addition to the long-term, veteran prisoners there were many emaciated, starving skeletons, sick people, and children whose survival was nothing short of a miracle.

I remember a crazy story that was told of Eulenspiegel,* that mad and mischievous character of folk legend. Eulenspiegel makes a heavy wager with the director of a hospital to the effect that he will cure all the patients within twenty-four hours, be they ever so sick and

---

* Till Eulenspiegel was the hero of a sixteenth-century book popular among peasants and artisans. Till was a trickster figure who triumphed over his "betters." Gerhart Hauptmann used the materials in his mock epic comedy of 1928; in 1895 Richard Strauss had used the same materials for his famous tone poem *Till Eulenspiegel.*

bedridden for ever so long. Then he goes to each individual patient and whispers in his ear: "The last one out is a dead man." The next morning he announces the evacuation and every patient jumps out of bed. Eulenspiegel wins the wager and goes on his merry way.

The buffoonery of a fool has turned into bloody reality. The march of the Auschwitz prisoners demonstrated what the human will is capable of doing when it is pushed to its limits.

Disgust

AFTER A SLEEPLESS NIGHT in the turmoil of the machine shed, the newly arrived prisoners were assigned to their blocks. A small number were transferred to camp blocks, while many others were relegated to tents. The temperature was barely above zero; only the densely overcrowded conditions in these makeshift shelters saved them from freezing to death. My group numbered about eight hundred, and all of us were assigned to the prisoners' detention block in Ravensbrück. A room meant to accommodate a maximum of 500 was already housing 645 German convicts from the Reich even before we arrived. All together, we swelled the numbers to a record 1,445.

Monstrous is the only word I can find to describe the inmates of that penal block in Ravensbrück—with the single exception of the evangelists.[58] The Nazis had delivered these believers to the concentration camp. The ones we met in the penal block in Ravensbrück had already served six to eight years there; even so, they remained unbroken and the strength of their faith shone in their eyes. They had continued to preach and distribute their religious tracts even in the camp, and it was these activities that had led to their confinement in the penal block. This detention center was strictly isolated from the rest of the camp and guarded by sentries and camp police. The other prisoners there were asocial elements, previously convicted prostitutes, jailbirds, and criminals of every description. They used us to satisfy their sadistic desires: for days on end we stood for hours on end shivering in the January cold, and even at night we were denied a spot to sit. If we tried to wash or relieve ourselves, we were beaten half to death.

The absolutely worst part of this existence was the food and the way it was distributed. The "imperial Germans" were first in line, and they ate their fill at our expense. Then we got our soup, in the same unwashed bowls the typhus patients and other dissipated, filthy, or infected prisoners had used and into which they had spit the chewed remains of stringy turnips. The series of one hundred bowls made the rounds again and again, unwashed and contaminated, each containing the waste left behind by one prisoner, to which was added the half ladle of soup for the next. Our spirits broken and our will rendered impotent by hunger, we emptied our bowls in turn with voracious gulps.

Why am I telling this disgusting story? Certainly not to upset the reader, but to give an indication of how far we had sunk. There is no saving face when caught up in the whirling dance of death. All inhibitions are cast aside. There are other things the very memory of which makes me sick—things in myself that I cannot forgive so easily.

I was quite fond of one of the girls who was with us on that march through the snow. She had just barely emerged from her sickbed, and the journey was far beyond her meager strength. She stumbled along laboriously and clung to my backpack for support. Exhausted beyond limit and hardly able to keep my own self up, I refused to drag her along. This girl, who managed to survive the train ride and arrived in Ravensbrück with an ulcerated inflammation of the mouth and severely swollen with the edema of starvation, was going to die anyway, and yet . . . If it had been my sister or my beloved, would I have helped, then?

The Liberation

ONE MIGHT EXPECT the liberation to be the brightest chapter in the history of the concentration camp. That's not necessarily true, at least not without certain qualifications.

We'd been waiting for imminent liberation from early April on, and we experienced every high and every low point of this vigil with excruciating clarity. Since every high point had to be paid for with many low ones, our spirits were more down than up. Many things spoke in favor of an Allied advance: the countless American and Russian fighter plane squadrons that circled above the camp, the exciting air battles that were played out over our heads, and the muffled pounding of the distant guns that gradually grew louder and closer in the nocturnal stillness. But this went on for weeks, in a constant but not increasing barrage. We had recently been transported to Neustadt,* a little town that didn't seem to exist on the map of Europe; wedged in between two fronts, it was apparently overlooked by both

---

* There were dozens of towns called Neustadt, literally "new town," in Germany. Without a more specific textual statement by Dr. Adelsberger, it is difficult to know whether the best candidate is Neustadt-Dosse, about thirty kilometers southwest of Ravensbrück, or Neustadt an der Glewe, about one hundred kilometers northwest of Ravensbrück.

sides, and us with it. Even if they were to search us out—Red Cross packages actually did reach us on April 12th—the Germans would probably make good their threat to bombard at the very last moment, leveling the camp and us at the same time.

The interminable waiting took its toll on our nerves. We had never been so impatient, not even through all the years with no hope of rescue. Veteran prisoners with overcompensating callousness became jumpy and irritable. Sleep was out of the question; we spent the nights straining our ears, listening in the void, noting every sound and registering the slightest oscillation and vibration in the immediate vicinity like a seismograph. Presentiments and nightmares produced rumors, and out of rumors developed chimeras that evaporated in thin air and hopes that burst like bubbles within a few hours.

On Monday, April 30th, we learned that the SS fighter pilot corps that was stationed all around our camp had been issued the following ultimatum: "The SS fighter pilot corps is summoned to surrender by 3 P.M. Tuesday afternoon and to land all planes at X on the other side of the Elbe." (We were never able to discover where X was.) We stood behind our wire fences, our eyes glued to every single movement the fighter pilots made; we were so excited we didn't even know whether the neighboring barracks had been evacuated or not.

Two days later—it was now May 2, 1945—the tension rose to a climax with the news that "Ravensbrück Concentration Camp, our main camp, has been liberated."[59] We were familiar with this announcement, for it had been repeated at least fifty times and in every conceivable variation since the beginning of March. But this time it really was true. The women overseers who had fled the camp brought the news personally in the early morning hours, and toward nine o'clock the camp leader gave a dulcet speech in which he confirmed the fact. He said something about the prisoners being consigned to the care of the Swedish Red Cross. He promised under sacred oath that not a hair on our heads would be harmed and, what's more, that he'd protect us from all danger and personally hand us over to the beneficent custody of the Allied forces. That was in the morning. By the time afternoon came around he'd forgotten all his promises or at least considered them superfluous; more important seemed to be his own safety. By three o'clock the otherwise so noisy SS vanished quickly and quietly from the camp, without attracting any attention.

At a quarter to four an American jeep manned by a forward patrol turned up. He was greeted with unbounded jubilation, almost smothered in exuberant embraces, and borne aloft on the shoulders of enthusiastic girls. In no time flat the jeep was bedecked with green boughs. Half an hour later he drove off and was soon followed by the liberating Russians.

And then what? A free-for-all for the arriving care packages, riotous plundering of the SS storerooms and whatever belongings the overseers had left behind, a wild tumult, with screaming, weeping, laughing, handshakes, and hugs, and amidst all this exuberance—an empty void.

A years-old yearning, a hope we hardly dared express even in our dreams, had actually come true—it was something even the most fanciful among us could never have imagined. We were incredulous and dumbstruck that first hour, when this inconceivable, unfathomable good fortune descended upon us. It was overwhelming, and it shattered us. Just as our starving bodies at first refused to digest the food they were now offered, so, too, were we unable to completely absorb our new freedom in those first hours. We had to accustom ourselves to it first, and we faltered along with clumsy, hesitant steps into our newly won life.

Gradually, of course, we did comprehend it. If I were to describe how we strolled through the beechwood forest during those early days in May, uninhibited and unguarded, and how we gazed through the tops of the birch trees to the heavens beyond, the heavens we could once again call our own, or how I stood in front of a blooming Japanese cherry tree and stroked the forsythia bushes with hands unshackled, and wandered through meadows bounded not by wires but only by the horizon, alone, free, and yet still connected to the wide world—if I were to describe all that, I'd have to be a poet: The heavens had opened.

Looking Back (Summer 1946)

I RECENTLY SPOKE with one of the aides associated with the camp relief work, a very intelligent woman with a great sense of responsibility. She has tended many former prisoners since the end of the war, including several Polish Jews who spent a few years in Auschwitz. She told me how distraught these girls still were as they wandered about in the world, the lone surviving members of their families and totally lost. Then she added, bitterly: "It would have been better had they not survived."

The sad part of this story is that she's not entirely wrong, at least as far as outlook and the joy of being alive are concerned. One or two years in the Auschwitz concentration camp took a heavy psychic toll on all its victims. Not only has the world around us changed, but we, too, have been remolded. Fairy tales and legends tell of angels and celestial messengers who were sent to Earth, lost their bearings, and couldn't find their way. Something like that can also be said of those who returned to Earth after years in hell. Human considerations and standards dissolved away. In the camp everything was disproportional and exaggerated in its dynamic, with the result that our thinking has changed and it's difficult to reaccustom ourselves to a normal routine. After so much brutality and so much cruel misfortune, one expects an excess of kindness and good fortune, and that's just not the way it is in this world. Sometimes, in the concentration camp, we used to talk about how life could never balance the books and restore what had been taken from us, even if it should offer us all the magnificence of the world. Our relations to other people and other things have been shunted along a different path. Perhaps we should look at it as a defect. Once you learn by painful, personal experience how everything vanishes—money and possessions, honor and reputation—and that the only thing that remains is a person's inner attitude, you acquire a profound disregard for the superficialities of life. We can't understand how someone who managed to slip through those years with his whole family intact, safe and sound, can waste so much as a word over the fact that his household isn't running like clockwork. We're astonished when a mother, whose children perished in unspeakable horror in Auschwitz, gets all worked up when her daughter's expensive jewelry, thought to have been in a safe place, can't be found. We can't even take seriously many of the things that burden our neighbors, because we constantly compare and remember how everything we once yearned for and fought for was wiped out with one stroke of a pen. We who had to watch 990 out of every 1,000 people die are no longer able—and this is a real defect—to take our own personal lives and our own future seriously.[60]

On the other hand, we take increased enjoyment in the little things of everyday life. After all that deprivation we consciously enjoy every slice of bread and every piece of cake. We treasure the warm coat that protects us against the cold; every single little amenity of life seems like a gift from heaven. We lap up the kindness of others the way a dry sponge absorbs water.

Sometimes we also reexperience the deep joys of our inner lives, when we hear the music of Bach and Mozart, when we see the flying colors of Rembrandt's *Night Watch,* or when the birds chirp and the sunbeams dance on autumn leaves.

Such moments are still rare, but even so they help us affirm life. It's a miracle and a gift of God that we survived Auschwitz; it's also an obligation. The legacy of the dead rests in our hands; it's incumbent upon us to tell their story. The telling of it is gruesome. Eyewitness reports of hell are not pleasant nursery tales; they are infernal and heartbreaking. It would be easier for all (and us as well) if we could touch them up a bit or never mention them again and forget it all. But that is exactly what we cannot do in memory of the dead.[61] The world must learn of their suffering, not so that the living should agonize over it or that it should embitter their lives, and certainly not for the sake of sensationalism, but rather as a lesson and a responsibility of future generations.

◆ ◆ ◆

THAT WAS AUSCHWITZ. I've tried my best to tell it as it was.

Non-Jewish Poles have wondered whether a memorial for the Jewish victims ought not someday stand in Auschwitz. It would be appropriate; for Auschwitz, with its three million martyrs, is perhaps the largest cemetery in the world. But there is a greater need for a different memorial, a memorial in the Horatian sense, one that is not bound to time and place. Auschwitz is, ultimately, only a part and only a symbol. There were other grisly places, Majdanek and Lublin, for example, in Poland, and many horrific concentration camps in Germany. And even if the number of Jewish victims exceeds that of all others, there are still more than enough of the others.[62] The masses of "political" Germans who were condemned to death must also be included in the tally. All of these victims cry out for retribution, but not the kind that comes with a stick in hand and hatred in the heart. Not, in other words, by imitating or modifying the sadistic methods we've come to abhor and reject from the very depths of our being. These dead demand a different revenge: the truth about Auschwitz. The world has to know that one small spark of hate can kindle an overwhelming conflagration that soon gets out of control. Then no one can extinguish it. There are some people who think these things could have happened anywhere in the world; I don't happen to share this view. But I can still remember the feeling I had when I read in *Eulenspiegel* how a man, bound to a bell clapper, was pounded to death and, in an Abyssinian book, how a rebel leader, wrapped in ribbons soaked in candle wax, was led to the stake: it was a supercilious sense of arrogance vis-à-vis medieval customs and inhuman attitudes. And yet, equally barbaric acts occurred in the very heart of Europe in the twentieth century.

A misguided fanaticism transformed civilized people into beasts who not only killed but tortured and murdered with joy and pleasure. A little bit of drawing-room anti-Semitism, some political and religious opposition, rejection of political dissidents—in itself a harmless mixture, until a madman comes along and turns it to dynamite. We have to understand this synthesis if the things that happened in Auschwitz are to be prevented in the future. When hatred and defamation quietly germinate, it's then, at that very moment, that we have to be alert and on guard. This is the legacy of the victims of Auschwitz.

The dead were strong; in their destruction they displayed a strength bordering on the colossal.

Can the living afford to be any weaker?

NOTES

1. The first decree restricting Jewish rights was issued April 7, 1933, but it was the Reich Citizen Law and the Race Laws promulgated at Nuremberg on September 15, 1935, that opened the floodgates and fostered the dozens of decrees and rules issued after June 1938. The decree mentioned here is the first of the Berlin decrees against "race mixing." For a rich sampling of the Race Laws and the decrees pursuant to them, see Lucy Dawidowicz, *A Holocaust Reader* (New York: Behrman House, 1976), pp. 35–142.

2. The Swiss government triggered the stamping of Jewish passports with a red "J" (for *Jude,* or Jew) by complaining of the immigration by Jews into Switzerland across a convenient frontier. The government made the complaint on June 28, 1938.

3. Three circumstances aggravated the visa problem: Swiss moves to restrict Jewish immigration; the Nazi decision to limit passports to six months' validity for Jews, producing situations in which, by the time a visa was obtained, the person's passport was no longer valid; almost all countries in the world passed rules or had unofficial policies to make it hard for Jews to immigrate. See David Wyman, *Paper Walls* (Amherst,

Mass.: University of Massachusetts Press, 1968); and his *The Abandonment of the Jews* (New York: Pantheon Books, 1984).

4. See Leni Yahil, "Rescue during the Holocaust, Opportunities and Obstacles," *Proceedings of the Eighth World Jewish Congress of Jewish Studies, Division B* (Jerusalem: Israeli University Presses, 1982), pp. 161–166.

5. Jews had formed a voluntary association called the Reich Representation in Germany in 1933. On July 4, 1939, by Gestapo decree the Reich Representation was forcibly changed into the Reich Association. Thereafter, each local Jewish Council was under direct Nazi control, and its agencies took orders and filled quotas issued from the Berlin Gestapo Central Office. Berlin housing was under the Jewish leader Hannah Kaminski.

6. Dr. Adelsberger telescopes events here. Whether to form ghettos or instead concentrated housing blocks scattered in the city was debated between Göring and Himmler. The decision was to implement systematic segregation, by legal decree. Thus, the Housing Council had no choice. All Jewish identity cards were marked, and the Star of David had to be worn on outer garments under a decree issued in September 1941. The diverse events reported by Dr. Adelsberger took place between November 1938 and early 1942.

7. These earlier deportations in 1940 generally involved camps within the Greater Reich. An exception was the brutal deportation of the Stettin Jews on February 12 and 13, 1940, to the Lublin-Lipowa Reservation in Poland. Of the 1300 deportees 280 died en route.

8. Here, again, the order of complex events, in which the exact chronology varied from country to country, is not made clear in Dr. Adelsberger's account. The Warsaw Ghetto was decreed October 12, 1940, and there were massive deportations under Göring's enabling decree of July 31, 1941. In Oslo, the deportations of all Norwegian Jews who did not escape to Sweden began on November 26, 1942. See Leni Yahil, *The Holocaust: The Fate of European Jewry* (New York: Oxford University Press, 1990), chaps. 11–14.

9. A "transport" was a train ordered by the SS from the German State Railway, Section 33 (Special Trains), for deporting Jews and others. The average "lading" was between 1,000 and 4,000. The SS paid fares to the Central European Travel Bureau at these rates: adults full fare; children four to twelve, half fare; children under four, free passage. The SS paid mostly in money confiscated from the Jews and other victims who were in effect paying their own fares to go to their deaths or to slave labor.

10. The phrase "sent to the East" always meant deported in one of the special trains, under the supervision of the General Director of the Eastern Line. Trains for Jewish resettlement often ranked higher than those for war materials, as the SS often gave priority to the "war against the Jews" in fulfilling Germany's "historic mission."

11. Dr. Adelsberger again conflates several distinct events. The date of her deportation was May 17, 1943, on one of the last transports from Berlin. The Reich had by then emptied Berlin of all but a few Jews. The deportation lists were supplied by the Jewish Council at Gestapo order. Dr. Adelsberger had been spared an earlier deportation because as a physician the Jewish Council needed her to care for the stricken Berlin Jewish community and had refused to place her on earlier lists.

12. SS is the abbreviation for *Schutzstaffel* (Support Squadron). Hitler had raised the SS to power as a counterweight to the Storm Troopers (*Sturmabteilung*). Himmler was named *Reichsführer* SS (Leader of the SS in the Reich) on January 31, 1929. This mere party formation, created as the guardian of racial ideology, became a true state-within-a-state: Richard Breitman, *The Architect of Genocide: Himmler and the Final Solution* (New York: Alfred A. Knopf, 1991).

13. The occasional use of passenger cars rather than cattle wagons for deportations to Theresienstadt and to the East in general is well documented, most readily in the interview with Walter Stier, who directed Section 33 of the German State Railway, and the commentary on

it by Raul Hilberg in Claude Lanzmann, *Shoah* (New York: Random House, 1985), pp. 132–145.

14. Ufa is the abbreviation for Universum Film A.G. (the initials A.G. stand for *Aktiengesellschaft,* a public limited-liability corporation). By 1936 Ufa was Germany's largest studio. Goebbels, head of the Propaganda Ministry, designed and executed its forced sale to the Nazi government as part of his purge of Jews from all media and his effort to gain total control over public expression. See David S. Hull, *Film in the Third Reich* (Berkeley and Los Angeles: University of California Press, 1969).

15. The main deportation route to Auschwitz via Breslau is well documented, from the first Berlin transport on March 26, 1942, in Martin Gilbert, *Atlas of the Holocaust* (New York: William Morrow, 1993). See maps 1, 164, and 184, and the commentary in the text. For an analysis of the system see Raul Hilberg, *The Destruction of the European Jews* (New York: Harper and Row, 1961), pp. 266–554.

16. Here Dr. Adelsberger describes the "selection" upon arrival of people sent to the right, deemed fit to enter the inmate labor population, and to the left, deemed unworthy of life and sent directly to the gas chambers. The judgment was made in the blink of the eye by Dr. Mengele and his assisting physicians. Those admitted and registered were subjected to periodic "selections" within the camps, by which the ill, disabled, and biologically exhausted inmates were chosen for gassing and cremation.

17. The footnote at p. 17 supplies identification only. Originally a labor camp for Polish prisoners, Auschwitz was expanded by the Nazis in three stages. First, on Himmler's written order of April 27, 1940, three hundred Jewish prisoners worked to enlarge the *Stammlager,* or main camp, to house the camp staff and several thousand prisoners. Then, by SS order in March 1941, the Nazis produced a huge camp about three kilometers west from the *Stammlager:* Auschwitz II, at Birkenau, which embraced nine specialized subcamps. A year later, a further order began the building of Auschwitz III, or Monowitz, a sprawling industrial and

mining enterprise six kilometers east of the main camp and embracing forty-five subcamps, including the Buna synthetic rubber plant and businesses using slave labor rented by the SS to I.G. Farben, Siemens, and other cartels. The combined population of all camps reached its high point on April 22, 1944: 105,168 persons. All gas chambers and crematoria were in the Birkenau sections, near the FKL.

18. These "tattoos" were in fact the inmate's registration number, preceded by a letter. Thereafter, inmates responded by number rather than by name. Being stripped of a name was a major step in the dehumanization that was a goal of the regime. Of about two million deportees, only 405,000 were ever entered into registers, signifying admission to the labor force.

19. All inmates other than Jews wore a simple colored triangular badge, the infamous *Winkel*. The color code included, among others, black for vagrants, green for convicts, red for politicals, pink for sexual offenders, and blue for Evangelicals. Jews had to wear a yellow triangle superimposed on a badge of another color, thus marking them with a Star of David. Most badges also displayed an inmate's number as well. The regime of random and deliberate violence depended on this system of colors and tattoo numbers: see Anna Pawelczynska, *Values and Violence in Auschwitz, A Sociological Analysis* (Berkeley and Los Angeles: University of California Press, 1979), pp. 83–93.

20. Gypsies (*Zegeuner*) were deported from throughout Greater Germany and from occupied or collaborating European states. Under the Race Laws they were officially "a plague" marked for eventual annihilation, with the inexplicable exception of "non-migratory" Gypsies. See Donald Krenick and Grattan Puxon, *The Destiny of Europe's Gypsies* (New York: Basic Books, 1972).

21. Here and elsewhere, "camp physician" refers to Dr. Josef Mengele. This is evident from a collation of Dr. Adelsberger's references to the "camp physician" on pp. 59, 63, 87, 88, and 95 of her memoir. Though she

never mentions Mengele by name, the activities described in these various references point to him only. Mengele had been a graduate student and then assistant to Professor Otman von Verschuer at the Institute for Racial Hygiene. Mengele's work at Auschwitz was described in correspondence with von Verschuer preserved in the U.S. Office of Strategic Services, R 73/15342m p. 64, column B. See Robert N. Proctor, *Racial Hygiene: Medicine under the Nazis* (Cambridge, Mass.: Harvard University Press, 1988), p. 44, where this document crucial to the identification of Mengele is quoted extensively.

22. Memoirs by other camp physicians corroborate Dr. Adelsberger's comments. See Louis J. Micheels, *Doctor 117641: A Holocaust Memoir* (New Haven: Yale University Press, 1989); Miklos Nyiszli, *A Doctor's Eyewitness Account* (Greenwich, Conn.: Fawcett Crest, 1960); and especially Gisella Perls, *I Was a Doctor in Auschwitz* (New York: The University Presses, 1948).

23. So-called revisionist historians scoff at reports of such huge killings and cremations in a single day. However, the capacity of the killing factory at Birkenau was 4,416 bodies a day without the use of open burning pits, which enabled the SS to kill and cremate as many as 12,000 Hungarian Jews during one day in 1944. See Arno Mayer, *Why Did the Heavens Not Darken?* (New York: Pantheon Books, 1990), pp. 366–368.

24. The initial landing was in Sicily, with a subsequent and very costly crossing to the "boot" of the Italian peninsula. The Italian fascist regime collapsed on September 9, 1943, but the Nazis then took direct charge of the continuing war. Rome fell to the Allies in June 1944.

25. The infamous *Appell* (roll call) described here was a central rite of the camps and is described in greater detail by the French survivor Charlotte Delbo, *None of Us Shall Return* (Boston: Beacon Press, 1978), pp. 26–34.

26. The inversion of normal reality was so complete in Auschwitz that many survivors later doubted the reality of the camp experience while also

insisting on their need to bear witness to the camp experience. See Terence Des Pres, *The Survivors, An Anatomy of Life in the Death Camps* (New York: Oxford University Press, 1976), chaps. 1–4. For a harrowing account of doubt see also Jean Amery, *At the Mind's Limits* (Bloomington: Indiana University Press, 1980).

27. The Norwegian Jewish population in 1941 was just over 1800 by actual census. More than 800 were rescued by the Underground (Milorg), with Swedish help. Of the 760 Jews deported to Auschwitz only 22 survived. This inmate death rate of more than 97 percent was the highest of any national group, perhaps because of a combination of Norwegian resistance to the Nazi invasion and occupation. The figures given are from my research in the Norwegian Royal Archives, Oslo.

28. On despair, on confrontation with the God in whom one believed on entering the camps but in whom faith was lost (loss of faith must be distinguished from loss of belief), see Elie Wiesel's accounts of his "argument with God" and of an actual "trial of God" by a rabbinical court of three believing rabbis who were inmates at Auschwitz: *The Night Trilogy* (New York: Noonday Press, 1985), pp. 17, 24, 30, 42–44, 53, 72–75, and 82–83.

29. Ethnic Germans were Germans born outside the Reich but considered "Aryans." Policy dictated that Ethnic Germans should be incorporated into the greater Fatherland as a matter of racial hygiene.

30. The expression "purchasing power" refers to the vast market economy in the camps. Prisoners traded everything from buttons and bread to cigarettes and stockings, especially for goods "organized" from the huge warehouses of goods called "Canadas" where the SS stored the confiscated goods of newly arrived deportees. "Organizing" meant stealing from the Nazis; theft from a fellow prisoner often resulted in a death sentence carried out by other prisoners.

31. It is unfortunate that this phrase may give support to the myth of the lack of Jewish resistance in ghettos and camps. Even in Auschwitz there

was organized Jewish resistance which was responsible for the destruction of Crematorium IV and the partial destruction of Crematoria II and III during a revolt on October 6, 1944. For more information on this event and the wider resistance in camps and ghettos see Lanzmann, *Shoah*, pp. 157–166; Philip Friedman, *Martyrs and Fighters* (New York: Praeger, 1954); Yitzhak Arad, *Ghetto in Flames* (Jerusalem: Yad Vashem, 1980); and the documents printed in Lucy Dawidowicz, *A Holocaust Reader*, pp. 329–380.

32. The Nazi practice of linguistic circumlocution and evasion of agency was systematic and not merely clumsy. For a close study of the way in which the language separated killers from any sense of agency in their actions, hence from responsibility, see "Language and Genocide," chap. 4 in Berel Lang, *Act and Idea in the Nazi Genocide* (Chicago: University of Chicago Press, 1990), especially pp. 81–102 and the extensive literature analyzed by Lang.

33. The Czech family camp B2B within Birkenau was unique. It was a special camp set up for more than thirty-five hundred deportees from Theresienstadt. Rudolph Vrba, a Czech Jewish inmate, worked in the Office of the Registrar and knew that the admission status of these deportees was peculiar because each had a file card reading "SB [*Sonderbehandlung,* that is, annihilation by gassing] after six months of quarantine." These Czech inmates of B2B were provided special quarters and special rations but were all gassed on March 7, 1944. See Lanzmann, *Shoah*, pp. 156–165, for the testimony by Vrba and Filip Mueller, a Czech Jew who worked in the *Sonderkommando*. This family camp seems to have been maintained for the deception of a visiting Red Cross team.

34. When Admiral Miklós Horthy, Regent of Hungary during the German occupation, refused to take special measures against Hungarian Jews, the Nazis seized direct control. Colonel Eichmann, the Gestapo and SS expert on deportations, went to Budapest to direct the deportation and

extermination of the Hungarian Jews. Deportations to Auschwitz began on May 15, 1944. Of a total Jewish population of 762,000, just over 445,000 were deported to Auschwitz and gassed and cremated. See Randolph L. Braham, *The Politics of Genocide: The Holocaust in Hungary,* 2 vols. (New York: Columbia University Press, 1981).

35. Here Dr. Adelsberger presents a part of a more complex whole. There were six killing centers on Polish territory. Four were exclusively death factories, with no permanent inmate facilities: Chełmno, Bełżec, Treblinka, and Sobibór. Auschwitz and Majdanek were both killing factories and slave labor camps. Lublin-Lipowa was a huge ghetto and reservation for Jews, and Majdanek was the death center for that territory. For a detailed account of these distinctions, see "The Extermination Sites," chap. 12 in Arno Mayer, *Why Did the Heavens Not Darken,* pp. 376–408.

36. Like the Czech family camp (see note 33), the Gypsy camp may have been used for "show" to impress the Red Cross in 1944.

37. Filip Mueller's vivid testimony from *Shoah* has been cited (see note 33). Mueller survived for three years as a member of the *Sonderkommando,* and his memoir provides a unique account of the grim work of this kommando. See *Auschwitz Inferno: The Testimony of a Sonderkommando* (New York: Stein and Day, 1979).

38. Three young girls employed in the German munitions plant at Monowitz smuggled explosives back to Rosa Robota, a sixteen-year-old Jewish resistance "organizer" (thief) who took part in the destruction of Crematorium IV and the disabling of Crematoria II and III in October 1944. Under torture by the SS, the munitions workers named Robota and she was hanged with them before an *Appell* of the whole Women's Camp: see Yuri Shul, *They Fought Back* (New York: Schocken Books, 1967), pp. 215–221.

39. Between the first Hungarian Jewish transport to Auschwitz on May 15, 1944, and the last on July 19, 1944, the average daily rate of gassings was

6,840. However, the capacity of the crematoria in Birkenau was less than 4,500, working around the clock. Hence, the Nazis resorted to mass burnings in open pits, using gasoline to fire the logs on which bodies (officially, "pieces") were stacked. See Randolph L. Braham, *Eichmann and the Destruction of Hungarian Jewry* (New York: Columbia University Press, 1961).

40. Dr. Adelsberger's language here recalls the great Rabbi Hillel's question: "If I am not for myself, who is for me? If I am for myself only, what am I?" *The Babylonian Talmud,* 35 vols. (London: The Socino Society, 1935–1948); Hillel's words appear in the treatise "Pirke Avot," 1:14 ("Ethics of the Fathers").

41. The day of the liquidation of the Gypsy camp. Hence, the day of the movement of medical personnel to other places, while Dr. Adelsberger remained in what became a camp for Hungarian Jews during the peak period of gassings and cremations.

42. This reference to experiments with twins is crucial to the identification of "the camp physician" as SS Dr. Mengele (see note 21).

43. The maintenance rules for inmates at Auschwitz dealt in detail with food, shelter, medical care, and, among other matters, the daily rental fee charged by the SS to large Nazi industries operating within the whole Auschwitz complex. The rules required that those slave laborers who became "used up" (that is, biologically exhausted) would then be "done away with" *(abgesetzt).* See Bernard Ferencz, *Less than Slaves* (Cambridge: Harvard University Press, 1979). Ferencz was one of the prosecutorial team in the Nuremberg trials of Nazi industrialists who had used slave labor.

44. Together with typhus, the main cause of death in the camps after their liberation. See Jon Bridgman, *The End of the Holocaust, The Liberation of the Camps* (Portland, Ore.: Areopagitica Press, 1990).

45. Deportations from Theresienstadt had been suspended from January 1943 through September 1943. Oswald Pohl, in charge of overall eco-

nomic operations in the conquered eastern territories, wanted to maintain the slave labor force for war production; the SS wanted the immediate liquidation of the Jews. When the deportations resumed, 25,375 of the 46,735 Jews sent to Auschwitz were declared unfit for labor and were immediately gassed. According to Theresienstadt camp records, 139,654 Jews passed into the camp and were registered, but on its liberation day the count of all Jews, in whatever condition, was 17,320.

46. Preparations to end the killing operations were under way in October 1944, as were plans to destroy all evidence, including paperwork, mass graves, and the gas chambers with crematoria. By December Himmler had issued an order to cease "selections," but gassings continued to occur until January 5, 1945. See the affidavit of Kurt Becher, March 8, 1946, *The Nuremberg Military Tribunals*, document PS-3762, in the U.S. Series of Documents.

47. This problem had three facets. Nazi eugenics dictated killing Jewish children and preventing live births as a means of ending Jewish existence by ending the reproductive pool. In the ghettos and camps Nazi regulations imposed the death penalty on mothers and known fathers. Eugenic principles and camp rules led Jewish secular and rabbinical boards to allow abortions, even to urge them, to preserve mothers' lives. Such urgings went against two millennia of Halakha (Hebrew for law). See Proctor, *Racial Hygiene*, pp. 96–125 and 198–205; and Hilberg, *The Destruction*, pp. 664–666. For ghetto decrees by Jewish authorities, see The Jewish Black Book Committee, *The Black Book* (New York: Duell and Sloane, 1946), pp. 331–333. On the vexing question of rabbinical interpretations of ancient law, see Irving Rosenbaum, *The Holocaust and Halakha* (New York: KTAV, 1976), for rabbinical interpretations.

48. *Mischlinge,* or Jews with some "Aryan" blood, had been defined by decree and were by further regulations allowed exemption from deportation according to the proportion of German blood to be "saved" for the future genetic pool of the Master Race. See Hilberg, *The Destruction,* pp.

50–53 and 268–277. The definitions appeared in the First Decree to the Reich Citizenship Law of November 14, 1935. The decree is printed in translation in Dawidowicz, *A Holocaust Reader,* pp. 45–47.

49. Dr. Adelsberger displays here the deference and admiration typical among inmates for "the low numbers," or those inmates who had survived in the camps for long periods of time.

50. The loss of the will to live was so common that in camp argot those doomed to selection because of it were called *Muselmänn* (singular) or *Muselmännen* (plural)—German for "Muslim." The individual *Muselmänn* exhibited characteristic signs: advanced starvation, apathy, and loss of the capacity to resist the camp routine, which was calculated to kill.

51. Daniel Rousset, a French survivor, coined the phrase "planet Auschwitz" to describe his experience. See Rousset's *The Other Kingdom* (New York: Reynal and Hitchcock, 1947), translated from the French *L'univers concentrationnaire.*

52. The Russians had overrun the easternmost camps, Bełżec, Sobibór, and Treblinka, by October 1944 but their advance stalled at the Vistula in early December. The last transport arrived in Auschwitz on January 5, 1945, when the camps were within Russian artillery range.

53. The Hungarian Jewish Councils and the World Jewish Congress had asked the Allies to bomb the rail lines to Auschwitz to slow the killing. The Allies refused. The bombing reported here must have been that of December 16, 1944, which was aimed at industry in Monowitz. The Russian bombings on January 12, 1945, near the I.G. Farben complex, were designed to soften defenses. On January 16, 1945, the Russians did shell the *Stammlager.* See Martin Gilbert, *Auschwitz and the Allies* (New York: Holt and Rinehart, 1981).

54. January 18, 1945, was the date of the last *Appell* at Birkenau. On that day, the Nazis, having destroyed what evidence of the mass killings they could, arranged the forced marches of more than fifty thousand of the

fifty-eight thousand inmates counted. See Bridgman, *The End of the Holocaust*, pp. 23–24.

55. The observation here is entirely accurate. Prisoners faced the decision whether to hide or undertake the evacuation that many thought would be death marches, calculating the survival value of the grim alternatives. The survival rate was lower among evacuees. On January 27, 1945, the Russian liberators of the First Perekop Division found about six thousand inmates alive in the Auschwitz camps. Many thousands died on the forced marches toward Buchenwald, Sachsenhausen, Mauthausen, and Dachau. See Wiesel, *Night*, pp. 85–91.

56. See Wiesel's haunting narrative of the death marches and the capricious killings en route in *Night*, pp. 88–102; for another account see Stefan Szwarc, "The March to Freedom," *Jewish Frontiers* (May 1948): pp. 11–15.

57. Ravensbrück, which lies about one hundred kilometers northnorthwest of Berlin, was established as a concentration camp in May 1939, on Himmler's order. By 1944 it had become a large women's camp holding thirty thousand inmates. This number grew as survivors of the death marches were registered in the camp early in 1945.

58. This account may be misconstrued. The convict population was a mixture of derelicts and other persons whose crimes were political—for example Communists, Socialists, Evangelicals, and Jehovah's Witnesses who resisted Nazism. The Evangelicals, especially, were marked for internment because of their active resistance to Nazi policy as early as 1935, under the leadership of Pastor Martin Niemöller. See Peter Mathieson, *The Third Reich and the Christian Churches* (Grand Rapids, Mich.: Eerdmans, 1981); Joachim Remak, *The Nazi Years: A Documentary History* (Prospect, Ill.: Waveland Press, 1969), pp. 100–101 (Niemöller's sermon); and the bibliography in Jacob Robinson, *The Holocaust and After: Sources in English* (Jerusalem: Israeli University Presses, 1973), items 665–669, p. 46.

59. Ravensbrück was evacuated on April 28, 1945, the day Dr. Adelsberger was sent to Neustadt. Negotiations to save about a thousand Jewish women had been successfully concluded between Himmler and Norbert Masur and Count Folke Bernadotte. It is likely Dr. Adelsberger was among the women thus saved. See Bridgman, *The End of the Holocaust*, pp. 29–30.

60. See citations from the literature on this theme in chap. 26, "Special Problems of Survivors," in Robinson, *The Holocaust and After*, pp. 186–189.

61. For discussion of this point, see Helen H. Waterford, *Commitment to the Dead* (Frederick, Colo.: Jende-Hagen Press, 1987). See also Pierre Vidal-Naquet, *Assassins of Memory* (New York: Columbia University Press, 1992); and Lawrence L. Langer, *Holocaust Testimonies: The Ruins of Memory* (New Haven: Yale University Press, 1991).

62. Disagreement persists on the total number of Jewish victims of the Nazi genocide. Raul Hilberg places the number at 5.1 million. See the revised and abridged edition of Hilberg's *The Destruction of the European Jews* (New York: Holmes and Meier, 1985), App. B, "Statistical Recapitulation," pp. 338–339. Hilberg's work is based on exhaustive research in demographic materials. At the other end of the scale, Lucy Dawidowicz places the Jewish dead at 5,933,900, estimating the total Jewish population within Nazi reach to have been 8,861,800. See *A Holocaust Reader*, App. 1, "Estimated Number of Jews Killed in the Final Solution," p. 381. The Nazi team working under Eichmann in 1942 estimated the European Jewish population in that year at over 11 million. This estimate was presented at the Wannsee Conference held in suburban Berlin on January 20, 1942. For a translation of the minutes of the conference made by Eichmann, see Dawidowicz, *A Holocaust Reader*, pp. 73–82.